MAN'S NEED

and GOD'S ACTION

MAN'S NEED
and GOD'S ACTION

REUEL L. HOWE

Foreword by

The Rev. Theodore O. Wedel, Ph.D.,

Canon of Washington Cathedral and Warden of the College

of Preachers

THE SEABURY PRESS · NEW YORK

Copyright 1953 by The Seabury Press, Incorporated.
Printed in the United States of America by the Colonial
Press Inc., Clinton, Mass. Designed by Stefan Salter.

Twentieth Printing
80-966-C-145-5

TO MY WIFE PEGGY

FOREWORD

IT HAS BEEN my privilege during the past few years to be associated with the author of this book in the presentation to clergy and lay folk of an invitation to a revitalized educational evangelism in the Church. In the form of lectures and informal talks, the material in this volume has been delivered scores of times. The content has gone through much evolutionary change and enrichment—a process which, as Dr. Howe says in his preface, is by no means at an end. But it has surely reached a stage of maturity that warrants a sharing with a reading public as well as a listening audience.

The presentation of the Christian Gospel, traditionally familiar to us, normally takes the form of proclamation. God has, according to Christian faith, acted in history, in Word, and "mighty act." The Gospel, in other words, begins with God and not with man. In an age of increasing religious illiteracy, however, proclamation of the Gospel requires prepared minds and hearts. Misunderstandings need removal. The "language of Canaan"

—of Bible and Creed and the Church's historic hymns and prayers—must be made relevant to life as modern men and women know it. Verbal presentations of the Gospel frequently find themselves giving answers to questions that have not been asked—or not asked as yet.

Can there, accordingly, be an approach to the Gospel which begins at the other end? Can we start with questions and not with answers? Can we lead modern men and women to face the mystery of themselves and their deeper hungers for salvation, often unacknowledged, for which the Gospel can then become light and healing? This pedagogic procedure looks dangerous at first. Dare we expose the precious truths of Christian faith to skeptical attack and doubt? Man is not God. Questions do not produce their own answers. Human need does not create divine revelation. God must be permitted to ask questions of man and not only man of God. Yet the method of correlating question and answer, human need and revelation, if tried in faith, may lead to astonishing results. Dialog replaces monolog. Doubts are brought into the light of day. Fake gods are exposed to judgment. Thus the drama of redemption of Biblical revelation can be seen once more to be relevant to all human life and not as a mere cultural elective for the pious.

Hundreds of those who have heard Dr. Howe's impassioned pleas for making the Gospel active in deed as well as word, in home and factory and office as well as in a compartmentalized activity which is called "religion," eagerly thank him for opening their eyes to the relevance of Christianity to daily living. As his insights now go forth between the covers of this book, may they continue to bring renewed understanding to minds and hearts prepared to rediscover the wonder and the glory of the faith of their fathers.

THEODORE O. WEDEL

PREFACE

As MANY of my readers will recognize, this book has grown out of the lectures I have given at the College of Preachers and elsewhere throughout the country where, with four other members of a team assembled by the Department of Christian Education of the Protestant Episcopal Church, an educational and theological retraining program was provided for both clergy and laity. For many years prior to this assignment I had been interested in the correlation of what we know about man with the truths of Christian theology. My teaching experience with the laity and clergy together with developments in my work with the students at the Virginia Seminary has hastened the process of correlation beyond anything that I had anticipated. I had expected to wait many years before attempting any serious publication of my studies, but the demand for this material has been so great that I have reluctantly consented to its appearance. I am well aware that I have not had time either to bring my thought to fuller maturity or to put it into as careful language as it deserves.

My attempts at correlation have been greatly assisted by the appearance of the first volume of Dr. Paul Tillich's *Systematic Theology*. In the introduction he describes his "method of correlation" as one which "tries to correlate the question implied in the situation, with the answers implied in the message." [1] Dr. Tillich, whom I do not know personally and under whom I have not had the privilege of studying, is in no way responsible either for my understanding of his method or for my use of it.

I offer the insights of this book to all who will read it with the hope that they will find understanding and inspiration for a pilgrimage in personal encounter wherein they will come to know and love both man and God more deeply.

For whatever value the following pages may have, I must make some acknowledgments. I am grateful, first of all, to my students who through the exciting years of discovery have been my teachers, and to my children, Marcy and Lanny, for planting my feet more firmly on the paths of understanding. With deep appreciation I acknowledge the very real interest and encouragement of Mrs. Ellason Downs in the preparation of this book. I am also very grateful to my friend and colleague, the Rev. Theodore O. Wedel, Warden of the College of

[1] Paul Tillich, *Systematic Theology* (Chicago, University of Chicago Press, 1950), p. 8. Copyright 1950 by the University of Chicago.

Preachers, for his companionship on the road, for his encouragement and criticism, and for writing the Foreword; and I am grateful to many other colleagues who have read and made helpful comments on the following pages. I cannot fail to mention my associate, the Rev. Barton M. Lloyd, who gave much time and devotion to a careful reading and criticism of my manuscript. He helped me greatly in the development of some parts of my thought, and through it all the reader will benefit from the value of his comments. To her to whom this book is dedicated there remains that blessing and help which while it can be appreciated can never be adequately expressed.

May we choose Him who has chosen us.

REUEL L. HOWE

The Virginia Seminary
Alexandria

CONTENTS

CHAPTER ONE

GOOD NEWS OR BAD?

"I SUPPOSE you wonder why I don't go to church. Why should I?" The question was asked by the husband of a member of my church. He had come to meet his wife, and while waiting we had fallen into conversation with each other. He is the head of an automobile agency, who has not only done well in business but is also active in civic affairs and is devoted to his family. After a pause, he went on to say, "I've got it pretty good—nice job, wife, and kids, and we're crazy about each other. We live in a good country and we have lots of friends. And look at the times we live in, too, with all the benefits of medical and productive science. If we'll only use our heads and play it right, we'll soon have a way of life that will make religion and church unnecessary."

He settled contentedly in his chair and smiled. I settled in mine and asked him to go on.

"You know," he continued, "I don't understand why you're in this church business anyhow. It would seem to me that you could get into something more alive and tied in with the real concerns of living. For the life of me, I don't see the point of what you're doing. Look at my wife who is one of your best members! She attends all these meetings, sometimes working herself to the bone. And for what? In order that some woman's group can raise five hundred dollars. Everybody rushing to and fro from one kind of meeting to another as if the devil were after them. My wife comes home completely exhausted and says, 'I don't know why I do it.' The other evening I asked, 'Well, why do you?' And she couldn't say a thing, but she looked at me with a kind of funny look as if for the first time she realized she didn't know.

"Sometimes she comes home all freshly steamed up with a new idea or program. I guess you sort of have to get up a new show now and then in order to whip up the enthusiasm and reserves of your exhausted faithful as well as try to arouse the disinterested like me.

"One of my pet peeves about your enterprise is the effect you have on my family. I spend a lot of my time when I'm home alone because you either have my kids or my wife trucking off to some meeting so that we're seldom home together. If I were mixed up in it, too, nobody would be home and I would be as frazzled as the rest of you.

"Look at you, you're run ragged trying to keep ahead of the show! While I don't believe much and don't go to church, I've often wondered why you don't organize and train your personnel better. It sure would save you a lot. No business could survive on the methods you people use.

"I hope I'm not being too hard on you, but while I'm at it there's something else on my mind. It has to do with the kind of lives religious people live in contrast to the kind of living they preach. I know my faults and I don't make any pretenses—I am what I am; but a lot of so-called church people pretend to be what they aren't. It seems to me that they're always looking down their noses at people that they think are not good enough to sit in the same church with them, to say nothing of sitting in the same pew. I don't want to have anything to do with the church until people in it are really as good as they pretend to be. I may not be much, but at least I'm not a hypocrite."

He subsided for a moment. Then looking at me out of the corner of his eye, he said, "My wife tells me I'm too outspoken and I've just come to realize I've been beating you over the head with my ideas."

"On the contrary," I replied, "You're saying things that need to be said. I'm wondering, though, what all this that you've been saying adds up to."

"I'm not sure, but there's something else that gets me about this religion business. You're always fussing among yourselves as to whom is right. We had some friends in the other night. One couple was Presbyterian and the others were members of your church. During the evening the discussion turned to some of the differences between you: low church versus high church, fundamentalists versus liberals, and so on. And then there was the question of who is right: the Presbyterians or Episcopalians or Roman Catholics. It all makes me sick! Why don't you get down to your real business, whatever it is?"

All of us have heard people both in and out of the Church talk like this man and raise his questions, or questions like them. I have used his conversation as a means of raising the questions to which this book is addressed.

He and others like him are rebelling against what we may call "churchism." Unfortunately, many outsiders are wrongly turned against faith in Christ because they are rightly repelled by churchism, parochialism, and sectarianism. Underlying such protests is an honest, though sometimes unconscious, question: "What is the real business of the Church anyhow?"

The simplest and most obvious true answer is that our real business is to preach the Gospel. "Go ye into all the world and preach the Gospel." But what is the Gospel? The Gospel is "Good News!" That is the meaning of the word. Again we hear a question, "Good news? What is the good news? We have not heard of any good news." Not only have people outside the Church not heard the good news, but many in the Church have not heard it either. They live not under the "good news" of the Gospel but under its bad news. The bad news of the Gospel is seen in the demand it makes of us. For instance, many people think that Christianity is imitating Jesus. Try it and discover that the effort to be like Him is most discouraging. If the Gospel is the demand to be like the perfect man, that is bad news.

Likewise, if the Gospel consists of keeping the commandment, "Thou shalt love the Lord thy God with all thy heart, with all thy soul and with all thy mind and thy neighbor as thyself," as pure demand it is the worst commandment of all. The effort to do that makes me so tense and anxious and perfectionistic that it becomes increasingly hard for me to keep the commandment. This kind of "Christian Gospel" says to me, "You have to keep the law in order to be saved." But I find that I cannot keep the law so I cannot be saved. This is bad news.

So we must try to give a helpful answer to these people who wonder what the good news is, or to people who ask for the good news. The simplest way to put the good news is that God loves us. The simplest and most profound definition of God is in St. John's Epistle: "God is Love." [1] The Gospel is the good news that God, Who is love, lived and died and lives again for us. It is not what *we have* to do but what God *has done!*

[1] I John, 4:16.

Now comes the next and most profound question, which again comes from people in, as well as outside, the Church: "Wherein is the Gospel good news—in relation to what?" For many of us, the answer to this seems obvious, yet for others of us it is not. The religion of some of us is not related to our lives. One man told me after he had discovered the relation between the two, "My religion, like that of many others, was like precious and fragile china which one has inherited, keeps in a safe place, takes down, dusts off and admires, but which one is afraid to use for fear it will be damaged, and which one keeps for posterity."

Since we so easily create conditions of loneliness by our anxiety, hostility, and distrust in relation to each other, we cannot hope to be the source of salvation. Nor can a religion help that commands "Thou shalt do the impossible," namely, live in perfect love and peace with God and man. As we have seen, this kind of religion is bad news for us. And if God's love is an answer to this problem, how is it an answer, and how may it become an answer for me?

Here it is! Here is the question for which we all want an answer. "How may the love of God be an answer for me?" I am going to try to interpret God's answer to this question in the language of today's experience. I know you want the answer now, neatly and conclusively. I am sorry, it cannot be given so immediately. It is the task of this whole book. Before the answer can become clear we will have to ask and answer other questions.

First, "What do you want? What do you *really* want? What moves you from day to day, week to week, month to month, year to year? What is it for which you would sell everything else?"

When we begin searching, we find that there are many answers. Some of our wants are immediate and superficial, some of them are deeper; but the deepest one of all is the desire *to be at one with someone, to have someone who can be at one with us, and through whom we can find at-oneness with all.*

Our desire for someone with whom we can be at one grows out of a profound loneliness. I do not refer to the loneliness of people who have not known love and who do not have friends; the deepest loneliness is that of people who have known love. If we are honest, we have to admit that though our experience of human love is partially fulfilling, it also creates a longing for a greater love than that which we have known. The full truth about human love, therefore, is that it both meets and does not meet our needs; that is, the more we have, the more we want. And this is more true of love than of anything else.

Each of us lives in a lonely place on the far side of the love we have known, and each longs to have those whom we love come and be with us there. Those who

would love us are hindered by their own unanswered
need of love and therefore cannot reach us in spite of
their longing to do so. Likewise do they live on the far
side of the love they have known, and they long for
us to be with them there; and no matter how we try,
we cannot quite reach them because of our self-con-
cerns. From the human point of view, this is the great
frustration. It is the frustration of being able to love
but not being able to love fully; the frustration of being
made for love and yet living a relationship which,
while it can give much, fails to give all that it promises.
Finally, there is the frustration of being unable to accept love, in spite of our deep need for it. We cannot
accept love because we are too worried about not being
loved, which is to say that we do not believe that the
love we really need exists.

Our loneliness, then, is in part a result of the nature
of existence, because existence itself means the separation of person from person, and such separation means
loneliness. I am a person and you are a person, and we
stand over and against each other in a state of separation, which is part of the experience of everyone. Dr.
Paul Tillich[2] points out that this state of separation is
a state of sin. We know that we really belong to someone and that somehow we have participated in the

[2] Paul Tillich, *The Shaking of the Foundations* (New York, Scribner,
1948), p. 155.

separation for which now we seek reunion. We can bring this meaning to the words of St. Augustine, "Thou hast made us for Thyself, O God, and our hearts are restless until they find their rest in Thee." Because Scripture and the best of our theological tradition teaches us that our relationships with God and man cannot be separated, a later theologian has changed Augustine's statement to read, "Thou hast made us for Thyself and for one another and our hearts are restless until they find rest in Thee in one another and in one another in Thee." [3]

All our life, therefore, is an effort to overcome our separation and to find each other in fulfilling relationship. Even strangers cannot pass on the street without being conscious of one another, and each looks to the other inquiringly with the unspoken question, "Would our coming together bring separation or union?" And how much a friendly encounter means, especially when we have not expected it; for friendliness means at least a partial overcoming of the separation that produces our sense of loneliness. Can we not admit that it has something of the quality of salvation in it? Indeed, looked at from the opposite side we can say that loneliness is Hell, and some theologians describe Hell as irrevocable and final loneliness!

[3] Herbert H. Farmer, *The Servant of the Word* (New York, Scribner, 1942), p. 39. Used by permission of the publisher.

We seek in many ways to overcome our separations and in so doing to find union with each other. We seek in marriage an answer to the cold loneliness of separation and mistakenly assume that our longings for union with one another will answer our deepest needs, with the result that people are disillusioned about love and marriage. If awareness that we cannot depend on our own self-centered and imperfect power of love helps us to recognize our need for a love that really has the power to reunite, then the relationship of marriage will become one in which reunion begins to be experienced. But if the shattering of illusions about love produces only despair, then the effect of the relationship will be increased separation and loneliness.

Many also seek to overcome the pain of loneliness that grows out of separation by their membership in organizations—civic, social, fraternal, and religious— each time hoping to find people with whom they can be close. These relationships can be helpful as long as we do not put full dependence on them to answer our deepest need.

Again, another effect of being separated from one another may be seen in the way we seek out anyone who will listen to us when we need to talk. And if the listeners have ears to hear, they hear people talk mostly about their loneliness and their sense of separation.

This is one reason why counselors are in such great demand. A sign of the state of relation in which we live is seen in the fact that only by paying can some of us find people who will listen to us.

There is also the loneliness that is the result of alienation. Sometimes our efforts to overcome our separation are made in alienating ways so that we accomplish the opposite of our intention. A friend of mine went to a meeting with the intention of mending a broken relationship by acknowledging his part of the difficulty. He did it, however, in such an arrogant way that he worsened the situation he had hoped to help. Sometimes when we go home from a party or business meeting we have to ask ourselves, "Now why did I do that? I am my own worst enemy." Many times we do these things but have no consciousness of them. Alienation is our way of living in our state of separation. We further estrange ourselves and each other from the very source and root of our being. And we need to notice how often we make others strangers as well as ourselves in relationships in which it is clearly intended that we are to be friends. We feel the contrast between what we are and what we might have been: We are alone but we might have been in relation. Later I will discuss more fully the effect of alienation in our lives.[4] Now I merely want

4 See Chapter Three.

to observe that the experience of estrangement increases
our sense of separation. A passage from a contemporary
novel gives grim but eloquent voice to our own need:

Naked and alone we came into exile. In her dark womb
we did not know our mother's face, from the prison of her
flesh have we come into the unspeakable and incommu-
nicable prison of this earth. Which of us has known his
brother? Which of us has looked into his father's heart?
Which of us has not remained forever prison-pent? Which
of us is not forever a stranger and alone . . . Lost! Remem-
bering speechlessly we seek the great forgotten language, the
lost lane-end into heaven . . . an unfound door. Where?
When? [5]

Much that has been said thus far shows our need
for living together in a relationship of love and trust.
We need the kind of encounters in which each gives
the other the freedom to be, in which each gives the
other acceptance and understanding. And the significance of this kind of relationship is that it is just as
important to be able to give as it is to receive.

Here again, however, we see the effects of separation
and alienation. The person who is lonely and feels unaccepted is not noted for his capacity to give himself to
those who need love and support. Does it not become
clear that we are involved in a vicious circle of need?

[5] Thomas Wolfe, *Look Homeward Angel* (New York, Scribner, 1929.)
Frontispiece. Used by permission of the publisher.

Man's need is for a relationship of love and acceptance, but when he turns to his companions for it, he finds that they too have the same need. Being preoccupied with our own needs and having little or nothing to spare for our neighbors, we turn away from each other, thus making our situation worse than before.

Because of our loneliness and anxiety resulting from separation and alienation from ourselves, each other, and God, *we want someone with whom we can be at one, who can be at one with us, and through whom we may find at-oneness with all.*[*] This is the deepest want of all, and the fact of our need is not at all dependent upon our being aware of it. All of us are moved by this desire whether we know it or not, and in one way or another we are seeking such a one, many of us in the wrong ways.

In relation to this need for at-oneness is the Gospel good news. God gave Himself in Jesus of Nazareth as the Personal Answer to man's need. Our task now is to understand and respond to God's action in terms of our need. By this means we will bring under critical review our present activity and behavior as Christians and churchmen with the hope of seeing more clearly what is our real purpose and mission. Our understanding of God's action will reveal to us who we are and what we ought to be doing. Out of our needs we will

* See Chapter Three.

ask deep questions. As we ask these questions, we will begin to hear His Answer. And as we begin to understand His Answer, we will be able to ask better questions that will lead to more comprehension of the ultimate answer.

CHAPTER TWO

THE ORIGINAL GIFT

WE HAVE BEGUN to see that we are lonely and anxious because of the separation which is characteristic of our existence and of the alienation characteristic of our way of living with one another. It has also begun to be clear that we need each other in a relationship that is mutually supportive and strengthening. How may we most deeply and fully understand the meaning of this fact?

The religious man understands the meaning of relationship in the light of his belief about God and His purpose in creation. God created persons and things (for what else is there?) to stand in a meaningful relation to each other and to Him. Indeed, this is our faith: God created us to live in relation to one another and Him, and we depend upon this structure of relationship for life and meaning.

The family is a good illustration of our dependence on one another. A baby at the moment of birth has the potentialities for personhood, but in order for *them* to be realized, it will be necesary for *him* to be accepted into the warm, welcoming, loving, and caring relationship of his family of persons—father, mother, brothers and sisters. To the degree that this is his experience he will become a happy, lovable, and loving person. To the degree that he is not so accepted, he will become an angry, frightened, and deformed person.

Recently, *Time* magazine under the heading "Medicine" gave a brief account of a study by Dr. Rene A. Spitz of ninety-one infants in a foundling home.[1] They had plenty of good food, clothing, light, air, and toys, and competent care. But they lacked one indispensable thing: the care by a mother. Each nurse had ten children, and as the report pointed out, "each infant had the equivalent of one-tenth of a mother, and this was not enough." Three months in this home was sufficient to produce marked changes in the babies' personalities. Checking on what became of the motherless foundlings, Dr. Spitz found that thirty per cent died in their first year and twenty-one, who survived their time in the home, were already so scarred by life that they could only be classed as idiots. He could get no data on the survival or emotional life of the thirty-two who were placed with foster parents.

Here is a dramatic picture of how important is a love relationship for mere survival, to say nothing of meaningful living. Another dramatic illustration of the role of relationship is to be seen in the many thousands of men and women, most of them young, who fill our

[1] *Time*, May 5, 1952. Courtesy of *Time*; copyright Time Inc. 1952.

mental hospitals to overflowing. Many of them are there because somebody did not take them in and give them a place in a warm and hospitable relationship. Somebody stiff-armed them emotionally; not intentionally, probably, but with such effect that they have run away from the cold ordeal of living with their fellow men. Nor must we think that these experiences are true only for orphans and mental patients. We all suffer the ill effects of exclusion—and we all exclude and hurt others.

There is temptation here to think that reference is being made to psychological, sociological, and pediatric insights, but if it is true that God created us to live in relation, then we are discovering a theological insight. In other words, it is God's will that we should live in a structure of persons in relationship with Himself and with one another.

One of the important conclusions that we have already drawn from this is that a person needs a place in such a structure in order to have a meaningful existence. It is impossible for us to exist apart from this world of the personal which includes man and God.

We need now to ask what this structure of personal relation means to God Who created it. As we read the Bible, we are impressed with the fact that in all the stories there is always the encounter between God and man. And as we look closer, we see that God is always speaking to men and through them to other men. When a man responds to God by saying "yes," then there is the accomplishment in the world of persons, and therefore in history, of the will of God; and when a man responds to God by saying "no," then the purposes of God are opposed by the egocentric purposes of the individual person. When I say "yes," then I find my *self* in Him and through my affirmative response He speaks through me to call to others. When I say "no," then I cut myself off from Him, lose the relationship without which I cease to be, and therefore cease to be an instrument of His speaking.

In brief, He speaks to persons through persons seeking to accomplish His purposes in us and through us. "God's purpose is such, and He so made humanity in accordance with that purpose, that He never enters into *personal* relationship with a man apart from other human persons." [2] "God's personal approach to men and women is always through other persons, or, more generally, through history which is the sphere of persons in relationship, the sphere where decisions have to be taken and choices made in relation with other wills." [3] The old *Israel*, the people who had a special relationship with God, existed as a witness to Him and as an

[2] Herbert H. Farmer, *The Servant of the Word* (New York, Scribner, 1942), p. 37. Used by permission of the publisher.
[3] *Ibid.*, p. 56.

instrument of His will among the nations of the world. His full revelation of Himself was in Jesus of Nazareth, Who was called Emmanuel, meaning "God with us"— that is, God with us in person to person encounter in order that we may be reconciled and reunited. And through Him we are the new people, the new Israel, the new structure of personal relationship—the Church —which is the instrument of His personal encounter with the children of men. More of this will be discussed later.[4] Now, it is in order to make our second conclusion about the importance of the structure of relationship, namely, that *in and through it do we meet and hear God and receive the blessing of His action.*

We have, then, this gift of relationship which has as its purpose the accomplishment of God's purpose for man, who is His creature and His child. As we look into the way in which we use this gift, we can see that we sadly misuse it. How else can we understand the state of life in our homes, communities, and the world? On the other hand, all is not black. We also see evidences of our longing and capacity for relationship, evidences of our faithful and cherishing use of the gift. The truest thing that can be said, then, is that our use of the gift is both faithful and unfaithful.

What happens in our lives when we misuse His gift

[4] Chapter Four ff.

and obstruct His purpose? Think about it this way: *God created persons to be loved*[5] *and things to be used.*[6] This is another way of saying that He created persons for personal relations with Him and with one another, and that the world of things was to serve a sacramental purpose, namely, to be the instrument of fulfilling relations between man and man, and man and God. Instead of loving persons and using things, however, we are always tempted to *love things* and *use persons.* What happens when we do this?

We love things! Why would I love things? Probably because my experience of love in relation to persons was disappointing and injurious. Many of us are afraid to love. We are afraid that our love will not be accepted, or if accepted, will be betrayed. "To love is to make oneself vulnerable" is a comment heard recently. "I will not give myself lest I get hurt" is another. As a substitute for persons I therefore love things because they will neither hurt me nor make a personal demand of me. Children sometimes steal things when they are not sufficiently loved; adults often seek consolation for disappointment in personal relations by the purchase of some "thing"—hat, car, rug, or anything.

[5] "You shall love the Lord your God with all your heart, and with all your soul, and with all your might," Deut. 6:4; Mark 12:30; "And your neighbor as yourself," Lev. 19:18; Mark 12:31.

[6] "So God created man . . . male and female . . . and . . . blessed them, and God said to them . . . have dominion over . . . every living thing," Gen. 1:27, 28.

Insofar as I am able to love, it is because I was loved, since I learn to love only by being loved. Because I learned to love by being loved, I expect the response of love when I love. But I love a thing, and things by nature cannot respond. Here is a car that can have much meaning for me, but only if I, or someone, operates it. But without me and my abilities the car can do nothing. Of itself it cannot speak to me or respond to me. When I love a thing that cannot respond, my act of love is frustrated since love is characteristically a person to person encounter in which there is mutual address and response. Such disappointments in response to acts of love drive us more despairingly in search of more "things" as compensation for not being loved, but this only multiplies the despair. The response to despair is suicide and murder, figuratively if not literally. Our communities and churches are filled with frightened and lonely people who, being afraid to give themselves in personal encounter, seek solace in the comfort of things, only to suffer from an increased sense of estrangement and death. And so we misuse God's gift of relationship and obstruct His purpose in our lives. We close ourselves to Him and to each other so that we are separated from each other more than ever and from any possibility of reunion. And yet our longing for reunion is so great that it drives us on to the search, but we seek in all directions except the right one.

Now there is the other way in which we misuse the gift of relationship. We *use persons!* By this I mean that I value and use what a person can *do for me* above what he *is in himself*. All men have functions: economic, social, sexual, and many other functions. We are dependent upon each other and should serve each other but not independently of what we are as persons. One of the things that is fundamentally wrong with our society is that its underlying assumption is that people are less important than the jobs they do; whereas, the true view is that men and women are essentially persons, meant to live in personal fellowship with one another, and that the services they have to perform in society are incidental and subordinate to this personal life.

We resent being used because we sense that we are losing our status as persons and are being forced into the role of things. This concept will help us to understand the evil of sexual promiscuity, and the problem of promiscuity in contrast to holy matrimony will help us to understand the evil of using persons. In sexual promiscuity the sexual function of another person is used to satisfy one's own self-centered needs irrespective of his significance as a person, that is, his function is exploited but he as a person is ignored and devalued. This cheapening of the person and exalting of his functions results in a demoralization that affects not only him but all who live in relation to him.

In contrast we have the relationship of holy matrimony in which a man and a woman love each other with a love that is a response to a deep and real meeting with each other. The experience arouses in each a sense of great blessing; and out of gratitude for the gift of love, each gives the other all his functions as a thank offering. Therefore, when meeting between them takes place in the sexual act, this becomes an outward and visible sign of the meeting of the two as persons in full communion with each other. In this we see a part of what we mean when we say that marriage is sacramental and call it holy matrimony.

When we use persons and treat them as things, we are hurting ourselves as well as them because we are engaged in an act of separation and estrangement. We were created for communication with each other, and the only real and deeply satisfying communication is that of love which unites and reunites. But to seek love is to lose it. When we seek *love*, people do not give it because they resent being by-passed and ignored for themselves and sought only for the love we want of them. Thus use divides, separates, and destroys relationship. Death, therefore, is the end for the man who *uses* rather than *loves* his neighbor, because in using he destroys the relationship in which God set him and upon which he is dependent for life. When my neighbor knows himself to be exploited by me, he naturally responds with resentment that easily becomes hate, the opposite of love. When I treat him as a thing, I make it more difficult for him to be a person. If his response is the natural one of resentment, then our relationship will be one of mutual estrangement in which we will experience both death in relation to each other and, to some degree, to all meaning.

Another aspect of the relation between persons and things and the role they play in our lives is seen in the fact that some individuals use both persons and things in a drive for power. One of the signs of the state of separation in which we live is the struggle for power in which we are all involved and by which we seek to achieve status and deal with inevitable feelings of inadequacy and loneliness. If we are successful in this struggle, we have both exploited persons and used things destructively with the result that our loneliness is increased and our status fails to give the desired feeling of adequacy. If we are unsuccessful in the struggle for power, we will have failed to exploit others successfully and will have become one of the exploited. Resentment of both our failure and the imagined success of others will further separate us from one another and from Him Who is the source of the life-giving relationship.

The struggle for power, which ends so disastrously, is a destructive turn of the drive for survival toward death. True survival of the individual is possible only in a relationship of love and trust in which the struggle for power is transformed into a life of achievement in a structure of mutual relationship. For this kind of life were we created, but it is obvious that we experience it only partially.

Thus, we see what happens when we misuse God's gift of relationship by loving things instead of persons and by using persons instead of things. The tension between persons and things is seen in the home where there are many moments when the decision has to be made between persons and property (things). Many peoples' feelings of inadequacy and hostility may be born of the choice that was made against them by their parents in favor of chintz sofas, china ashtrays, furniture, painted walls, and so on. Parents who brag that their children never broke anything in spite of the fact that they kept their houses furnished just as they were before the advent of their children would do well to ask themselves what they might have broken in their children during the process. This same choice between persons and property increases the more complex our culture becomes. Housing developments in the interest of property maintenance limit the number of children and their activities; many toys are made not to last too long in order to increase sales regardless of children's heartbreak over the loss of something of value to them.

The gift of relationship is given because only in the community of the I and Thou can personality arise. "A person makes his appearance by entering into relation with other persons." [7] Only as I am confronted by others can I become a person and participate in the most characteristic act of persons in relation; namely, communion. And yet as we have seen, we have responded to this gift in ways that make us subpersonal in our relations to each other and produce separation and death.

[7] Martin Buber, *I and Thou* (Edinburgh, T. and T. Clark, 1937), p. 62.

1.29.19 —

CHAPTER THREE

THE WORST HURT AND
THE BEST HEALING

GOD'S GIFT of relationship with Him and with one another, with all that it promises of fulfilment, is denied us by our sin. We can understand this sin as being our assertion that we are sufficient of ourselves, that we do not need relationship with God and man. Even more, our anxious seeking for our own being keeps us from finding our being in Him and in our relations with one another. We fear men and hurt them, and exploit not only persons but things so that both the world of persons and the world of things become the instruments of our self-destruction. So pervasive and powerful is this perversion within us that even our religion and our religious observances can become the servants of alienation and death. Even the bread and wine of our salvation can become the bread and wine of our egocentric shattering of love and peace, and our altars can be altars of separation rather than altars of reunion of that which is separated.

Our task in this chapter is to face and accept the fact that our ability to achieve reconciliation ourselves is hopeless because we are both alienated and alienating. Many of you will recoil from this point of view and ask,

"Why is it necessary to go into this sort of thing? Isn't it better left unrecognized and undealt with? After all, did you not say that we're going to seek to understand better the Good News?"

How I wish we could evade this task, but since we cannot, how glad I am that we have help for facing it! Do we not see that the good news cannot be good news to us unless we have a sense of the bad news of our own situation? Much preaching of the Gospel is without power because it seeks to give people a good news who have no sense of their need for it, because the answer of the Gospel is given to people who have not been helped to ask the questions that make the Gospel the necessary, indispensable answer.

But we have a comfort and a strength for the facing of the task: We would not dare face it were it not for the God Who made us for Himself and so for each other, and Who has acted to save us from the very situation that confronts us. He offers us a security of a new and saving relationship—the nature of which we will seek to understand later and without which we would have to withdraw from the task at hand.

We now pick up the theme of alienation as the source of our difficulties in relationship where we left it after a brief introduction in Chapter One. There we identified alienation as the act of separation. Indeed, the worst hurt any of us can experience is the hurt suffered at the hands of someone we love and from whom we expect love. There are other hurts that we seek to avoid or flee from, such as physical injuries and injuries resulting from the loss of money, job, or property. But bad as they are, they cannot and do not hurt us as seriously as personal hurts. Personal hurts hurt on the inside; the others hurt on the outside. Inside hurts are more injurious than outside ones because, as we have seen, we are dependent on one another; and when we have been hurt by another person, there is the feeling that we have been cut off from him, with the consequent anxiety that to a greater or lesser extent we will cease *to be*. This is the real fear of death. So personal hurts have life and death significance.

Before going further in this discussion, we need to recognize that we respond to what men do to us with more or less readiness to be hurt. Some of us are hypersensitive and are easily hurt. Others of us, because of a securer sense of self, are not so easily threatened. Our susceptibility to injury, however, in no way relieves us of our responsibility to treat each other considerately. In fact, it ought to increase our sense of responsibility, as we shall see later in this chapter, because our hypersensitivity indicates a need that ought to be met in the interests of our future capacity for relationship. Our proneness to feel hurt in human encounters and our consequent need to be on guard in human relations are born out of our earlier experiences with significant people. They are results of not being accepted and loved in times of crisis when our dependence on these relationships was most acute. We may not have been loved or we may have been loved falsely for ulterior reasons, not loved as persons but used as things.

The loneliness and anxiety caused by this kind of treatment increases and causes us to find various ways to protect ourselves from others and to avoid the destructive consequences to our self-esteem and sense of security. For some, physical illness becomes a means of protection from the threatening encounters of life; retreat from the real world into the world of unconscious fantasy is another; extreme passivity or aggression may keep others from feeling too vulnerable; alcohol, drugs, inordinate eating may be the refuge of others; extreme sexual interest and activity help others from facing how deeply they have been hurt; and, of course, murder and suicide are the final efforts of all attempts to protect ourselves from the hurt of human encounter.

The power of the experience of rejection is such that it is possible for us to be hurt by persons so grievously that we become person-shy. In any mental hospital, for instance, we can see people who have been hurt so seriously that they have retreated completely from the world of persons and sit day after day, year in and year out, folded up in the foetal position not moving nor hearing nor seeing. They had lived once in the world of persons but with increasing difficulty and pain until, at last, the hurt became so unbearable that they retreated back over the way they had come, seeking that place where they had been most secure. And it is an indication of the state of relationship in their lives that they found no resting place until they had retreated back into the womb. Once in a while through patient care and encouragement over a long period of time one of these retreated souls can be drawn out enough for him to take a very timid, tentative peek at the world of persons again. One unfriendly move, though, sends him back again.

We do not have to look in the back wards of hospitals to find the casualties of human encounter. Otto Will writes of one young boy from a "good" family, for instance, who "knows the aloneness and the growing terror, the living in a world peopled by those who listen but do not hear, who speak but do not communicate, who demand affection but do not give tenderness, who invite closeness and cannot tolerate intimacy, who smile and frown and sneer and laugh in a fashion perpetually and hopelessly inappropriate, who insist that they love but do not notice the pain of the loved one, who encourage the accomplishment of the impossible, who proclaim that there is hope while their own lives so clearly act out despair. He knows all this so well that he has come to live on the alert, expecting to find in all humans that destructiveness which he found in a few. It is not difficult for him to discover in many of his fellows some characteristic threateningly remindful of his humiliations with people—and once such idiocrasy (temperamental peculiarity) is noted he does not long pause to see what else a man may contain, but is aware only of fear, suspicion, and the need to run." [1] This is how badly a person can hurt a person. This is the work of alienation.

There are three ways in which we experience alienation: In relation to oneself, to others, to God. Much of the discussion thus far has illustrated the alienation that takes place among us. There is also the rejection that one experiences in relation to oneself. "I do not feel that I am all that I was meant to be" is a comment often heard from people who are disappointed that they have not better realized their potentialities. Again, "I do things that I do not want to do, and want to do things that I do not do. In fact, I seem to be at least two different people, if not more, and these different persons that I am do not like each other." Many of us, along with our inordinate self-love, have feelings of hostility toward ourselves. If this surprises you and you want to reject the thought, pause a moment before you do and

[1] Otto Allen Will, Jr., M.D., "'Data' and the Psychiatric Patient," *Journal of Clinical Pastoral Work*, Vol. II, Summer, 1949, No. 2. Used by permission.

recall those things that you have done on occasion that resulted in hurt to yourself. The hurt may have been physical due to your carelessness, but your lack of "care" of yourself could very easily be and often is an act of hostility on your part toward yourself. Insurance investigators have an interesting story to tell about the purposefulness of many accidents, and the self-hating and self-destroying purpose is prominent among them. As a result of various experiences of life, we all have antagonistic feelings that constantly seek expression. Not daring to express them in relation to others, and lacking adequate means of dealing with them creatively, we may turn them in upon ourselves. Or our hurt may be social. We speak and act in ways that cause others to speak and act against us.

Earlier, we saw that the separation between ourselves and others was intolerable, and we sought by one means or another to effect a restoration of oneness. Our response to separation within ourselves is to be seen in the thoughts we think and the things we do to find peace of mind or soul. We want to be "at one" with ourselves. All too often our efforts produce only a superficial peace, while contrary feelings and purposes battle for control. As the prodigal son, who realized that he was still the father's son even though he was far from home, feeding swine and eating their food, finally "came to himself," we, too, long to come to ourselves.

"Integration of personality" is the modern psychological phrase for the same interior at-oneness.

A third aspect of our separation has to do with our alienation from God. We feel ourselves separated from Him in "Whom we live and move and have our being"; we feel alone, unaccepted and unacceptable, anxious, and finally, hostile. The lover's passion to lose himself and yet be found in the beloved describes the yearning of the isolated human soul to be gathered up into the fullness of being. The deepest significance of religion has to do with our attempt, through rites, ceremonies, feasts, fasts, and the meeting of ethical demand, to mend the break between ourselves and our God. Here, too, we want to be "at one" with Him Who is the "ground of our being."

Unfortunately, however, much "religious" activity, ceremonial or otherwise, does not have reuniting effect. Long has it been known to the sensitive and discerning that we can easily use religion to keep people at arm's length, to prevent real encounter between persons and thus become the instrument of brokenness rather than reconciliation. Religious activity of various kinds can be and often is an expression of hostility.

We have gradually approached a word which is one of the most important words in the theological vocabulary: "atonement." The word is important because it expresses the object of all of life—the desire for at-one-ment; the reuniting of everything that is separated; the reconciliation of man with himself, of man with his neighbor, and of man with his God. And I feel that the meaning of this word, even partially or superficially understood, makes clear the deepest meanings of all human behavior. All men seek to effect a reunion of the separated and a reconciliation of the alienated.

Children's behavior is often revealing at this point. An interruption of the usual feeling of closeness between Judy and her mother gives Judy a feeling of separation and anxiety. This state of partial being or not-being on Judy's part is probably due to something she has done that makes her feel unacceptable. She therefore feels that she must do something to restore herself to union with her mother. She may come in bringing her mother a gift by which she hopes to propitiate the mother and gain her good will. On another occasion she says, "Mother, I'm sorry I was bad. From now on I'll be a good girl." The intent here is that on the basis of promise of future goodness the mother will take her back into warm, loving relationship. Or, Judy may try to effect restoration by self-punishment, and shut herself in her room. Much of our behavior has to do with our attempts to achieve a reunion of the brokenness of our lives. The tragic aspect of our behavior is that it does not achieve what it sets out to do. We cannot restore the life we have destroyed. The restoration, as we shall see later, comes by the gift of God's love, which alone can restore.

But two insights begin to come clear: The first is that our need for reconciliation and restoration is desperate, and the second is that, while there is nothing that we can do that will undo the alienation and close the separation we have caused, the only effective healing for person-hurts is person-healing. What other kind of healing can there be? Since we were made for relationship with God and with one another, the hurt of alienation remains unhealed until touched by the healing of a new and, this time, accepting relationship. Children's direct responses illustrate this truth. When they are hurt, they run to someone they trust and literally throw themselves into healing arms; and when they emerge, often all is well. There is profound truth in the cry: "Kiss it, Mommy, and it will be all better." Nor should we think that the need and availability of this kind of therapy should pass with the passing of childhood. Some months ago a physician writing in *The Atlantic Monthly* about his experience undergoing an operation without anaesthetic reported that even the accidental touch of the human hand was sufficient to penetrate and relieve the terrible isolation and loneliness that he experienced in a world of pain.[2]

[2] Fredric Wertham, M.D., "A Study of Pain," *The Atlantic*, Vol. 189, March, 1952, No. 3.

We do not need to go to such extremes to find illustration of the prevalence as well as the necessity of person-healing for person-hurt. To whatever degree there is true regard and love for others, person-healing occurs. The difficulty is that our capacity for hurting another far exceeds our capacity for healing. I have to face the fact that I can so hurt another that he will never again be accessible to me, and, as we have seen, perhaps to others or even to himself. This is to kill! When I face such a one, assuming that I have only seriously wounded him and not destroyed him, and seek to heal him, assuming again that I am repentant, I am confronted with obstacles in the way of helping him. First there is always in me that concern for myself that stands between me and a selfless concern that is necessary if I am really to help him. Second, there is in him, based on his self-concern, a justifiable defensiveness and mistrust of me. Even my efforts to help him may, because of our respective conditions, further alienate us from each other. Multiply this kind of situation, over-simplified as it is, unlimitedly and you have a fractional basis for understanding the profound complexity of the state of men's relationship.

Only one conclusion is possible: I cannot save myself; you cannot save yourself. Who can and will?

We can begin to understand anew the meaning of God's action in and through Jesus of Nazareth. The

Being of God made Himself known in Jesus through a living face-to-face encounter with men in order that He might bring to our person-hurts His Infinite Person-healing. At one of our laymen's conferences, a man said to me, "I've never understood why God would undertake a business as big as salvation through just one man in one little place and in such a limited way." Once we begin to understand the principle of person-healing for person-hurt, seeing it operate in a limited and broken way in our own lives, then the reasonableness of God's action in these terms becomes apparent. How else could it be done? Certainly, the impersonality of a program or a movement of some kind would not have met such personal need. No, God's answer, as always, is appropriate to the need. Christ Himself identifies His mission for us. He refers to Himself as a physician,[3] and says that He came to heal the sick,[4] and to seek out the lost.[5]

As He lived with men they were powerfully drawn to Him; and as they were drawn to Him, they were drawn to one another. This was a new kind of relationship—something they had never known before. As this Divine Person lived and died and lived again (for sin and death had no power over Him), the conviction grew in them that they were beginning to experience a new kind of relationship, and at Pentecost there came

[3] Matt., 9:12.
[4] Matt., 8:7.
[5] Matt., 15:24.

into the world something wholly new and unique. The Spirit of this new relationship indwelt them and they found themselves participating in a new creation, a new order of redeemed personal relations set in the midst of the old broken order, continuing the action which was begun through the Incarnate Person.

St. Paul described that action: "God was in Christ reconciling the world unto Himself." The word reconciliation is just right for what we have been talking about. God's answer to our alienation is His reconciliation. Reconciliation is the business of the Church. As the new relationship created by the Spirit, we are set in the world to bring the *Gift* of God's reconciliation. "Therefore if any one is in Christ, he is a new creation; the old has passed away, behold, the new has come. All this is from God, who through Christ reconciled us to himself and gave us the ministry of reconciliation; that is, God was in Christ reconciling the world to himself, not counting their trespasses against them, and entrusting to us the message of reconciliation. So we are ambassadors for Christ, God making his appeal through us. We beseech you on behalf of Christ, be reconciled to God." [6]

If there is anything that we are doing as individuals or as parishes that does not fit into this reconciling purpose, then it is not our business; and if there is any-

[6] 2 Cor., 5:17-20. From the Revised Standard Version of the Bible. Copyrighted 1946 and 1952.

thing we ought to be doing that fits into it, then we must make it our business.

Here is one way to combat the enervating effect of churchism and orient our thoughts and activities to the true and great issues of life. Some of the superficial and irrelevant concerns of church life are due to the absence of an effective criterion by which we may evaluate our individual and corporate Christian witness. Reconciliation is one of the key words for understanding the purpose of the Christian ministry, which belongs as much to the laity as to the clergy. Reconciliation is, therefore, a simple single criterion for rethinking our ministry. What is the effect of our way of living with one another? What happens to people in our church meetings? What is the effect of our church's witness in the community where it lives? Is it alienation or reconciliation?

CHAPTER FOUR

THE GIFT OF THE
NEW RELATIONSHIP

THUS FAR in our discussion we have seen that the Gospel of Jesus Christ is *good news* to lonely and anxious men whose loneliness and anxiety are due to the loss of relationship that is needed to nourish our being. Our experiences in relation to each other both hurt and heal, both take away and give a sense of being. Every experience of life has in it the possibilities for alienation, destruction, and death; and also of reconciliation, fulfilment, and life. In brief, we may say that every human situation is one in which there is tension between life and death. The issue is not life *or* death, but life *and* death—which means that our situation is never so good that we are not the victims of daemonic forces working both in us and on us, nor so bad that there are not the possibilities of life and redemption.

A very simple kind of illustration is to be found in the situation that is created when one is asked to go elsewhere to live and work. The first response may be one of enthusiasm and anticipation, but in a few days these will probably be succeeded by second and more sober thoughts. They may run something like this: "I know my situation here. In some respects it is not as good as I would like, but at least I know what to expect in the way of deprivation, absence of opportunity, painful relationships, etc.; and I know also the assets here. As for this other place, it looks good now, but in a year or two what will it produce of good and ill for my wife, my children, and me? But even more important, what will it offer in the way of opportunities for service to God and man?" Again and again in our lives, especially in our momentous decisions, we have to weigh the question, "What will this mean, more life or more death?"

Nowhere are these conflicting possibilities more clear than in the eight most fundamental and crucial experiences of human life: birth, growth, maturity, mating, parenthood, sickness and other crises (such as unemployment, loss of money), bereavement, and death. These are the common ventures of life to which all men are called and to which, if they live, they must make some kind of response.

Each of these holds promise of life and death for all of us. Birth, for instance, which seems to suggest only the possibility of life is commonly referred to as a "blessed event," but have we not seen times when it set parents against each other? If a child is not wanted, or not wanted at a particular time, or not wanted for the right reason, his birth may be an occasion of separation, of destruction, and of death. Many people wish that they had never been born. This can only mean that the birth of such a person was far from being a blessed event and was instead more destructive than life-giving. Or here is a young couple coming in love and with hope to their marriage. Will this experience be one that will produce a sense of deep communion and union or will they come to know chiefly loneliness and anxiety? So, in all of these common experiences of men, we see the promise of life and death.

We speak of these experiences as times of crisis when men must make decisions, and back of decisions are the great questions. Therefore, we may conclude that the deepest questions that men ask about their existence and its meaning grow out of these moments that are so clearly identifiable, that have so much promise for good and ill. Most religions have addressed themselves to the deep questions that men ask out of these crucial moments of their living. This is outstandingly true of Christianity.

For the opening event of human life, birth, with its implicit question, "How shall I find the full meaning of life?" Christianity offers the great initiatory sacrament of Holy Baptism, by means of which we are re-born into the relationship that has the promise implicit in the phrase "Child of God."

For the experience of growth, which calls for repeated crucial decisions for the human child as he passes from one stage of development to another, there is the ministry of instruction, carried on by both the language of words and the language of relationship.[1] This is part of the Christian Church's response to the obligations assumed at the time of baptism.

For that dramatic transition from childhood to adulthood (adolescence), the Church offers the rite of Confirmation in which God gives added strength to us who, as we assume responsibility for our own decisions and way of life, need a guiding and strengthening Presence.

For mating, in which man and woman coming out of separation are looking for deep communion and union, the Church offers Solemnization of Holy Matrimony, which says that the only full and true reunion of that which is separated is to be found in Him Who triumphed over the self-love that would always separate and alienate you from one another.

For parenthood with its implicit question, "Who is equal to this responsibility?" there is usually some rite or ministry that makes clear that our finite and sinfully impaired resources for what seem to be infinite responsibilities need the redeeming and completing power of the Divine Father.

[1] For a discussion of the phrase "language of relationship" see Chapter V.

For sickness, which itself stands as witness to the destructive and daemonic forces of life, there is offered the healing of prayer,[2] which changes the center from self to God. The life of prayer is one in which I lose my life, and in losing it for His sake find it, and in finding it regain health and vitality, though not necessarily accompanied by remission of symptoms.

For bereavement and death with its implicit question, "Is this all?" there are the rites and teaching that affirm faith in being in the face of human non-being.

Thus, through this ministry, the Church seeks to bring to each of these human experiences the resources of grace that will help people to make their decisions on the side of reunion, fulfilment, and life. It will not be possible to go into a discussion of all these ministries as fully as I should like, but it is my intent to give rather full attention to the sacrament of baptism and its meaning for our life.

First of all, we need to understand that a sacrament is the means of God's action and that through the sacrament of Holy Baptism we become Christians. It is not through our initiative that we become members of the Christian Church but through God's. Not by our joining but by our being joined is our membership achieved. Since baptism is the instrument and symbol

[2] The ministry to the sick may include the Early Church rites of Unction of the Sick and a Laying on of Hands.

of the new relationship that we have with one another and with Him, it is basic to every other ministry that the Church performs; indeed, every other ministry gathers its meaning from the basic meaning inherent in baptism. Even the Holy Communion cannot be understood except in terms of the Holy Community, which is created by the Holy Spirit through Holy Baptism. In other words, baptism is the cornerstone upon which the whole structure of the Church and of the Christian ministry is built. Although I shall have much to say about the baptism of infants, yet all that I say will apply equally well to adult baptism.

Canon Quick identifies baptism as having two significances: first, the instrumental; and second, the symbolical.[3] In baptism God acts instrumentally at the time of the rite while we are standing around the font. The relationship of this child to God as His child is declared and sealed so that he is received as "a member of Christ, a Child of God, and an inheritor of the Kingdom of Heaven." That this is the meaning of baptism we accept on faith. It is not that our faith makes the action or makes it true; it is true, and our faith is our relation to the truth. But our faith needs to be translated into action.

This brings us to the second aspect of the meaning

[3] Oliver C. Quick, *The Christian Sacraments* (London, Nisbet and Company, 1944).

of baptism, namely, the symbolical one. By this I mean that what is done at the font points to future action. As Canon Quick puts it, "More is begun than is at the moment effected." Instrumentally, as we have seen, the new relationship that the child has with God and with his new people is declared and sealed, but this is only a beginning. Along the same line Martin Luther writes: "The sacrament, or sign, of baptism is quickly over, as we plainly see. But the thing it signifies, namely, the spiritual baptism, the drowning of sin, lasts so long as we live, and is completed only in death." [4] It is the intention of the sacrament, of course, that this new relationship should be realized not only by the child but by the participants in his baptism. Every baptism is a reminder of our own baptismal relationship into which we receive the child and out of which we hope he will emerge conscious of and participating in his identity and heritage as a child of God. We need to remember that that which is to be effected is still God's action, which He seeks to accomplish in part through our baptismal relation to the child. Here again we meet the concept of God acting in and through men. He trusts us to be faithful not only *to* Him for each other, but also *for* Him to each other.

The service of baptism itself points to this future action, to that which is to be effected. For instance, after

[4] Martin Luther, *Treatise on Baptism.*

the act of baptism has been accomplished, we pray that "this child may lead the rest of his life according to this beginning." Earlier in this service we promise that we will do some things in his behalf, namely teach him the "Creed, the Lord's Prayer, the Ten Commandments, and all other things that a Christian ought to know and to believe to his soul's health." In later chapters (Six, Seven, Eight), I shall discuss what we mean by these promises, but my present purpose is to indicate that at the time of baptism itself we point to the things that we, the baptizing fellowship, are required to be and do in relation to this child in the name of the Triune God in Whose Name he is baptized.

The continuing action of baptism is to be recognized not only in the care and instruction that immediately follows the act, but in all the ministry of the Church from now until the earthly life of the newly baptized is finished and his body laid in the ground. Even then, the fellowship of the redeemed follows him with their prayers and memorials into the life on the yonder side of death. The baptismal relationship is an eternal one.

Our immediate concerns, here, however, have to do with the beginning of this continuing action. "Baptism, with its inseparable symbolic and instrumental aspects, standing at the beginning of the Christian life, on the one hand signifies a state of salvation which is fully reached only through the whole process of life, and on the other effects forthwith the necessary first stage of that life." [5] It is clear that if the newly baptized is to realize the meaning of the act for him, someone will have to live with him, and for him, and even *"die"* for him. This is the vocation of our baptismal relationship to him, but the baptismal relationship is more than just our human relationship under a new title. If this were all, it would be of no more effect than initiation in any club or other organization. It is the new relationship that conveys the power of God in Christ for salvation—a relationship of the redeemed and the redeeming; of the forgiven and the forgiving; of those who freely give out of what they have freely received; of those who, having surrendered themselves, have become the instruments of His saving love; of those who, though broken and sinful, by Him are used to heal and save. This is what it means to be His Church, the people of God, the new order of redeemed personal relationship, the reconciling fellowship.

Thus the continuing action of baptism needs the baptismal fellowship of the Church. As Dr. T. O. Wedel points out in his exposition of the Epistle to the Ephesians, "No man can be a Christian by himself. We meet Christ in the fellowship." [6] And the child's

[5] *Doctrine in the Church of England* (London, S.P.C.K., 1938), p. 137. Used by permission of the publisher.
[6] *The Interpreter's Bible* (Nashville, Abingdon-Cokesbury, 1953), X, 612. Used by permission of the publisher.

fellowship in which he may meet Christ is his family, if the life of that family is lived in Christ. The fellowship of persons living in relation become mediate agents of God's action. That God acts in and through men is difficult for many people to accept. Yet, if belief in the Holy Spirit means anything, it means in part that He enters into personal encounter with men who when they say "yes," are purified, illumined, and transformed by Him and become His personal representatives. Thus we may with confidence affirm that whoever is in Christ and guided by His Spirit is an instrument of the meeting between God and man.

Therefore, when the Church promises to be the vehicle of the new relationship in baptism, who are the responsible persons? The minister? The difficulty here is that the child is not as intimately and constantly accessible to him as the language of relationship requires The minister as a baptized member of the Church, as well as an ordained leader, does have a responsibility for the child, of course, but it cannot be met for the time being in a direct, face-to-face way. For some years, because of the child's inaccessibility as an independent person and learner the minister will have to exercise responsibility by his guidance of others who are also baptismally responsible, and who have direct personal access to the child.

Among these others are the god-parents, but there

are many in the Church who no longer believe that a god-parent can serve in the ways intended because people move about the country so frequently and readily that the possibility of a continuing accessible relation-ship is not certain. The mobility of the population cannot be doubted, but the conclusion that sponsors can no longer be useful should be questioned. The sponsor or god-parent should be a baptized practicing Christian who has a special interest in the child and is willing through the years to assist the parents and others in his care and instruction. He will seek to bring to the child's experiences a relationship of trust, love and understand-ing that will awaken in the child the response of love, trust, and integrity. And, finally, the sponsor will seek to make him aware that he is dependent upon Christ for both the image of what, as a child of God, he is meant to be, and for the help to attain to that "mature manhood, to the measure of the stature of the fullness of Christ." [7]

Undoubtedly this concept of the role of the sponsor will discourage many who have assumed the responsibility as well as those who might. And yet even a towering concept that at first glance seems to overwhelm may in the end be helpful. For instance, many god-parents are bored with their task because the office and

[7] Eph., 4:13. From the Revised Standard Version of the Bible. Copyrighted 1946 and 1952.

the little things they do are lacking in greatness of meaning. The Bible that you might give your godchild is not an end in itself but rather a symbol that points, for the child and all men, to the encounter of man and God through the ages; that points to His action on our behalf, of which your relationship as sponsor to your godchild is a local contemporary expression. The meaning of this will be developed further in Chapters Six, Seven, and Eight. We need to remember, also, that as sponsors we have responsibility not only for our own charges but for all the children of the household of faith. Because of the nature of the promises made at the child's baptism, sponsors should expect to serve as teachers in Sunday schools or other Christian educational enterprises or contribute in any other way to the welfare of children generally.

On the other hand, it should be pointed out that sponsors or witnesses do not carry their responsibilities alone. While they are designated to serve in the name of the Church of Christ in order that certain individuals will be clearly responsible, they also serve to remind all of us of our duty to these children. Among those to whom they point as responsible people in this baptismal relationship are parents, to whom children are obviously accessible and who, of course, already have a natural and profoundly meaningful relationship.

The whole Church, therefore, is responsible: the

minister as a member and leader of the fellowship, the sponsors as members and representatives of the fellowship, the parents as members and as persons in relation to whom the child will have his first experience of relationship. In this baptismal relationship of which Christ is the foundation, the child will be held and nourished as he becomes a "new creature" in the "new creation." And let us not think of this new baptismal relationship as being parochial. Far from it! I am not baptized into the Roman or Presbyterian or Episcopal Church but into the universal Church of Christ. Baptism means that we are all related to each other in Christ and therefore responsible for each other in His Name.

We need, however, to look microscopically at our responsibilities before we scan them telescopically. For this reason we turn to a study of our more face-to-face relationships in which the child will be awakened to the meaning of the new relationship in which he stands.

CHAPTER FIVE

THE LANGUAGE OF THE NEW RELATIONSHIP

WE HAVE the gift of the new relationship from God in Christ into which baptism is the door. He gave us this gift not for ourselves only, but for all men. The Christian Church exists primarily for those who are not in it, which is to say that our chief aim is missionary. The first meaning of baptism for us is that we are cared for, but its second meaning is that we are called to care for others; first we are ministered unto, but finally we must minister. How easy it is, however, for us to think of the Church as existing primarily for those who are already in; how easy it is for us to be concerned for our parish's success, prestige, and adornment and to forget those to whom we are sent. We may be so forgetful of our mission as to resent any reminders of our responsibility to those outside and to resent, also, their intrusion into our "fellowship" when they appear as a result of others' invitations. On the contrary, the Christian's mark of maturity is his readiness to seek out and care for or minister. All of us having been baptized are ministers of Christ, both laity and clergy.

All natural relationships offer natural opportunities

for this ministry, and none more completely than the parental one. And certainly, if the rite of baptism is to be followed immediately by the beginning of the process that is to effect all that was begun, then parents, in the case of infants and children, are key people. When we study the natural role of the parents, we begin to see how profoundly they are ministers and how much depends upon them.

In the first place, the relationship is a primary one. With the parent, the child has his first experience of relationship that will profoundly determine his capacity for relationship thereafter. Anyone who has ever worked with people cannot help but see that our capacities and incapacities for living with others grow out of our earlier experiences of relationship, particularly the primary one with our parents. And why not? How else would we learn to live with one another? It is not surprising, for instance, that difficulties in the marital relationship often grow out of difficulties that the partners had in relation to their respective parents. A boy who had been constantly criticized by a perfectionistic mother will be unable as a husband to enter into a relationship of mutual give and take with his wife. He will brood over even just criticisms because he will be unable to discuss them with her. Similarly, difficulties in any relationship go back, in part, to the casual influences of the first relationships. And I would not exclude from this influence of family experiences the individual's future capacity for relationship with God. Of course, God has power to transcend and redeem the effect of these, but as we have seen, relationship on the human level may open or close us temporarily to a relationship with God.[1]

Likewise, the role of a parent in relation to his child is important because in the very early years the child does his most significant learning. Some educators say that all basic learning takes place before the sixth year and that all later learning is but an elaboration of the earlier. We cannot be sure that this is true; but if there is any possibility of its being true, would it not be wise to act as if it were? If it is true, then we will have taught helpfully and well. On the other hand, if it turns out not to be true, no harm will have been done. Certainly, we can agree that during these early years the child acquires indelibly ideas, motives, values, feelings that will have a profoundly determinative effect upon his character, and which in later life will be difficult to change.

An illustration of one of the results of these early influences is that a child acquires a sense of trust and mistrust by the time he is twelve to fifteen months old. Dr. Erik Erikson refers to this as "basic trust which I think is an attitude toward oneself and the world de-

[1] See Chapter Four.

rived from the experiences in the first year of life."[2] Our sense of trust and mistrust is concerned finally with our sense of self in relation to others who are the source determinative in the realization of our being.

Basic trust is fundamental to all trust relationships including those that we call religious. Trust is trust, and who can distinguish between trust and faith? The experience of basic trust in the early years of life is, as we shall see in a moment, a foundation for the later capacity for faith in God. From the beginning of life to the end we must walk by trust or faith (call it what you will) in someone, man or God, and preferably in both.

We see, therefore, how deep a sense as trust is awakened so early in the life of a child. And yet many religious people, many church people, have been heard to say that there is not much that we can do in the way of Christian teaching until a child is old enough to go to school and has a fairly well-developed capacity to use and understand the language of words. If we hold this view, we do not really understand the role of relationship in education, and we put too much stock in what can be accomplished by means of words alone. The assumption that teaching is done primarily through verbal communication is still fairly common. Back of this as-

[2] Erik H. Erikson. "Growth and Crises of the Healthy Personality," from *Problems of Infancy*, Hilton J. E. Senn, ed. Josiah Macy, Jr. Foundation (1950), Supplement II. Used by permission.

sumption is another one: that words have meanings within themselves. If this were true, we could engage in a conversation and never have difficulty with the meaning of words. We would always understand one another; and if one of us introduced a word that was new to the other, understanding would not be impaired because the word itself would communicate the meaning or could be explained simply by other words. How wonderful that would be! And yet how ridiculous is the possibility of its being true. We know how easily a discussion becomes confused because we do not have the same meaning for our words.

Herein is the answer to our problem! The meaning is not just behind the word but also in the understanding of the person using the word. An obvious example is in our different understandings of the word love. The preacher is talking to his people about the love of God. One man who has gone through the depths in his relations with his wife and children and emerged confident, faithful, and accepting, brings his meanings to what he hears about the love of God. Another man is unhappy and sick because he has not yet found someone who can be affectionate with him and not make any demands of him, and therefore he brings very inadequate personal meaning to the understanding of the meaning of love. Also in this congregation is a young girl for whom the word love means a chum. People bring meaning out of their experiences in relationship for their use and hearing of the important words.

Back of the word, therefore, is its meaning; back of its meaning is the experience of men living in relation. The encounter between man and man and man and God produces the experience that has a meaning that demands a word as a permanent symbol by which all like experiences may be identified.

Let us use the child's acquisition of trust as an illustration. In the first place, he did not acquire it through the verbal affirmation and explanations of his mother. She did not sit her child on her knee and say, "Listen, my child, you must understand that I can be trusted. I am really quite trustworthy. There is this evidence and that evidence that I am a trustworthy person. Please believe that I know who you are, what your wants are, that I'll take good care of you. Please say that you know I am to be trusted." All the child would do in response to this frantic verbal attempt to preach the gospel of trust would be to stare uncomprehendingly at his anxious mother and acquire from her not a sense of trust but a sense of anxiety communicated by both her increasingly anxious effort to teach trust and by her failure to provide the very relationship that would awaken his trust. I wonder if we do not do just this when we endeavor to preach the Gospel of Christ by means of verbal affirmations, assurances, and explanations alone?

How then did the mother teach basic trust to her child? First, one does not, cannot *teach* trust. Trust can only be *awakened* in a person. Little is accomplished with untrusting people by talking to them about trust or by giving them books to read on the subject. After the trust is awakened, then they can be instructed through words, books, and other resources.

But how was it awakened in the first place? It was awakened by the mother's demonstration of trustworthiness. The newborn infant is only potentially a person and begins life in a state of complete dependence. He is dependent upon mother, father, and other members of his family. Through them, he is dependent upon the whole culture for food, care, love, and guidance. His first contribution at this time, if not his sole one, is represented by the phrase "I want." If he is to survive, to say nothing of prospering, his wants should receive the response of personal attention. Why should we make such response to the baby's wants? Is this not indulgence and therefore unchristian? This might seem to be the case were it not for the fact that *back of the want* for food, for companionship there is a need and hunger for all that makes possible life and being. We need to see that the calling of an infant into being as a personal self cannot be done apart from meeting his wants. Only in this way can we have meaningful personal encounter with him. When the baby is hungry, therefore, he must be fed. When he is wet and cold, he must be made comfortable. When he is lonely, he must have companionship. Satisfaction of want, at first simple and later more complex, gives the individual a feeling of well-being which leads eventually to a feeling of being loved, and that the loving one is to be trusted. The mother, having a sense of vocation for the well-being of her child, ministers to his needs so dependably that in a very short time he has had an experience the meaning of which he might put this way if he could talk: "I am beginning to know who you are. You are someone upon whom I can depend." In this way there is gradually awakened in him a sense of trust.

On the other hand, the mother is human. She cannot be in two places at once. She has other children and a husband. She has times of weariness and irritation. Accidents happen over which she has no control. Because of these conditions, in addition to other and deeper obstacles to the complete meeting of his need, she is not as dependable as he would like her to be and needs her to be. And out of the experience of deprivation and disappointment and unfulfilled wants of all kinds, come the meanings to which we have to give the word "mistrust." There are many lonely, anxious, and alienated people, who, though they may use the symbols and ceremonies of a religion of reconciliation, do not and cannot enter into a trust relationship with God or man.

Years ago a man said wistfully to one of my students: "I wish I could believe that God is God." He expresses for thousands and millions of us the longing of our souls. He uttered a prayer that calls for an answer. Implicit in it is the question, "How do you awaken trust?"

We awake it not by use of the language of words alone but by the use of another language as well, a language which if rightly used is more basic. This is the language of relationship, the language the mother used, the language of mutual address and response, the language of trust and love. It is the language by means of which life provides children with experiences that make it possible for them to respond to the deepest and most complete personal meanings and to call them forth from others. The use of these two languages needs to be correlated because when we have awakened in another the response of trust, anything that we may teach about trust will have meaning for him, and he will be able to learn more about it through verbal instruction.

There is abundant evidence that the Church in carrying on its teaching function has put too much faith in the use of words and used too little the language of relationship. The result is that people are not helped to understand the meaning of their own experiences or to bring these meanings to the understandings of the meanings of the words used in preaching and other methods of formal teaching. The teacher is equally re-

sponsible for the relationships out of which come meanings that are essential to the child's future understanding and way of living. Children also need our
help to formulate the meanings of their experience so
that these will be available for further learning. As we
shall see more fully later, these personal meanings need
to be completed and made more universal by being
united with the deeper and larger meanings that have
come out of the best experience of men through the
centuries.[3] The word should be the instrument by which
this is accomplished. A word is a symbol, and it should
point to both the meanings possessed by the individual
and to the meanings of the race. For example, the religious word faith should be the symbol of the meanings
the child can bring out of his experience of basic trust,
and also the symbol of the affirmative meanings that
come out of the experiences of people in their encounters
with God. The child's trust-meanings need the larger,
deeper, and more complex meanings that lie back of
the word faith in the experience of the people of God.
In order for words to have this power of conveying the
meaning of the fellowship to the individual, it is necessary for the fellowship to assume relationship responsibility for the meanings the individual should bring to
the hearing of the word.

This insight is at the heart of the meaning of the

[3] See Chapter Six.

promises of the Church to teach the child the Creed, the Lord's Prayer, and the Ten Commandments. As we shall see in succeeding chapters, more is intended than mere memorization of the words or even the transmission of the meanings that tradition has given the words and forms. Equally important, because without it the words and their traditional meanings will have no contemporary force, is the necessity for the meaning of the child's experience to be available as a point of contact for the new meanings symbolized by these verbal forms.

Our need today, therefore, is to be able again to speak through the language of relationship as well as through the language of words. I need the grace to *be* in order to help my child, my wife, my friend, my student to *become*. And what do I mean when I suggest that your becoming is dependent upon my being? Simply this: my friendliness helps you to become friendly, my trustworthiness helps you to become trustworthy; or my hostility causes you to become hostile, my anxiety causes you to become anxious. If I affirm, you will become affirmative. This is what I call the language of relationship, the communication that results from living together and which gives us the basic and personal meanings for the words we hear and use. The spirit of the relationship determines the nature of the communication. The partisan, self-righteous spirit, which brings into being a mob, communicates bigotry and hatred for all who do not agree. The Holy Spirit, Who brings into *being* the fellowship of love and reconciliation through that same relationship, provides the experiences that causes us to *become reconciled* and to *be reconcilers*.

Thus, the Spirit gives the relationship in which meaningful communication takes place. The Spirit, therefore, makes our relationship a language, a means of engendering being and communicating meaning.

Here is a way of understanding the importance of the parental relationship as a means of teaching and upon which partly depends the realization of the meanings of baptism. Parents are the child's first teachers and the teachers upon whom the child must depend to provide the first and basic instruction. As instruments of the Church's pastoral and teaching function, parents need help in understanding the opportunity inherent in their parental relationship and in accepting their need of the Spirit to help them *to be* in relation to God in order that they may help their children *to become*, in fact as well as in name, "children of God." To this we shall turn our attention in the next chapter.

CHAPTER SIX

GOD'S LOVE AND OURS

THUS FAR we have recognized man's deepest need as the need to be "at one" with someone, and we have shown that the Gospel is the answer to this need. And since this need grows out of a sense of alienation that exists within and between men, as well as between man and God, our task as the Church is to bring God's reconciliation to men.

We have considered how Christian education can be carried on, and we have concluded that the cornerstone of the Church's ministry (and this includes the ministry of teaching) is the sacrament of baptism. We have seen that the full action of God is not to be found in that which is done around the Font, because more is begun there than is at the moment effected. The full action of God in baptism has to be completed by the later action of God through the Church in relation to the child or person who is being baptized.

Who then is responsible for that which is to be effected? Who carries on the Church's ministry? We saw that parents exercised a crucial role during the first years of their children's lives. The importance of their role is seen in the fact that in the first twelve months of life the child may acquire a sense of basic trust that becomes his not by being lectured to about trust and mistrust, but by his experience of the dependability or trustworthiness of those who minister to him. His trust is awakened by the parents' "language of relationship" which provides the meanings that are necessary for any later "ministry of the word."

In this sense, therefore, parents are important ministers of both the Church's teaching and pastoral ministry at a very crucial time. We now face the task of describing how that ministry may be carried on.

We must not think that the ministry which will be discussed in the following pages is a ministry that can be carried on only by parents. The use of the parental relationship has a two-fold purpose: first, to explain the parental relationship in terms of its possibilities for expressing the ministry of the Church; and second, to use it as an illustration of the fundamental characteristic of *any* ministry whether by layman or clergyman. For all ministry is primarily a ministry of relationship or it cannot bring men into saving encounter with the redeeming God. All of us need this salvation, and all of us are needed for this ministry of salvation.

Our *need* and our *being needed* are intimately related to each other, and God's answer is related to both as we shall now see. The approach to the understanding of God's action will proceed from a study and understanding of man's need. More often the study of religion proceeds from the top down; that is, we first seek to understand Who God is and what He is doing and then proceed to an application of this understanding to our own situation. In this study we shall proceed from an understanding of human need to an understanding of God's action as the Divine Answer to human need. We always need to remember, though, that both approaches are necessary. An understanding of the human situation apart from the Gospel is impotent. But the Gospel apart from an understanding of its relation to the human situation is meaningless.

Second, in further considering man's need, we need to be more specific. Our need for someone in and through whom we can find "atoneness" will now be studied in the light of our needs for love, for acceptance, and for discipline. We will discuss these as though they were separate needs; but when we have finished, you will probably conclude that they are three aspects of one need. They must, however, be dealt with as though they were separate in order to make the meanings clear. First, we come to our need of love.

A child needs the constant assurances and reassurances of love. He needs to be loved in order that he may love himself, and loving himself be able to love others who also need love. Love of self here has the meaning of our Lord's commandment: "Thou shalt love thy neighbor as thyself," and is distinguished from egocentric self-love. Only those who have been loved and who love themselves are free and able to love others. The ability to love is always the result of having been loved. This is true in the child's relation to the parent, and it is true of our relation to God. We read in the first Epistle of St. John: "Herein is love, not that we loved God, but that He loved us . . ." [1] Love is always a response to being loved, and this brings us face to face immediately with the second great responsibility of the Christian Church, which is to be a community, a community of love.

The need of love is desperate because without love we die. All men, since they need love so desperately, demand love of us and demand perfect love; but we demand it of them, too. We cannot meet such a demand, of course, because our own egocentric preoccupation with our need of love finds the love demands of others unwelcome and too demanding. While love is supposed to be spontaneous, the effect of our self-demand is to make love a labor, and we are not always equal to the arduousness of the relationship. We romanticize and sentimentalize love, or we idealize our love longings and betray ourselves into thinking that our power of love is greater than it is. Loving one an-

[1] I John, 4:10.

other is not easy. The infant does not immediately know whether he is loved or not loved. He is not born into this life with the ready-made capacity to love. He has potentialities to both love and hate, and the issue depends on whether or not someone wants and *loves him.* If we begin life by being loved, the experience of being loved awakens in us a capacity to love, gives us such a sense of being that we have the necessary security to endure not being loved, which is an inevitable experience of life. The final capacity of love is to love those who act against us and appear to be our enemies. All men who have known love at all are under the vocation to love their enemies.

How do we first experience love? Our first experiences of love are intimately associated with our experiences of being fed. When the baby wakes up, he is hungry. Hunger to the infant is experienced as pain, and he cries for an answer to his pain which, of course, is food. The simple act of giving food because of the ease of discomfort and the gift of satiety that it can effect is an act that has tremendous potentiality for the communication of meaning. When he wakens to eat in response to hunger pains, he becomes aware of the world in which he lives, and he becomes aware of the important people in his life. His important people are those who meet his needs, particularly his need for food. And the way in which they give him food is as important as the food because it tells him how his mother, and therefore the world, feels about him. If she is glad to see him, enjoys his being awake, holds him long and close to her, talks and sings to him, he associates these expressions of love with the food that eases the physical pains of hunger. Not only does this set up a deep association between food and love, which is to play an important part during his life, but food becomes for him a sacrament of his *being* and of his relationships. In every culture that we know anything about, we see this sacramental relation between food and fellowship.

The ultimate of this association is to be seen in the Holy Communion, which we may truly regard as the sacrament of the common food and the uncommon love. It is as if the Redeemer, wishing to find some means, outward and visible, by which He could symbolize and preserve the experience of love, reached back into His act of creation and used that which He made true there, namely, the association between food and love. So He took bread and wine, the common food of His time, which fed the bodies of men and was the vehicle of their fellowship, and made them sacramental instruments of the new relationship, the uncommon love of God. As a pastor, I have had people come to me with the complaint that the Holy Communion did not mean as much to them as they thought it ought to mean. I used to think that if I gave such a person a devotional manual on the Holy Communion, his difficulties would be solved. I found, instead, that the difficulties not only persisted but often grew worse. Then, quite by accident I discovered his problem originated from within his own life and had to do with his experiences in relationship. I remember one person in particular, a man who, as he talked about himself, unfolded the story of a good deal of dissension and contention within his family, with much of it centering around the family table. An intimate knowledge of the family bore out the story that much strife and conflict had accompanied feeding during the first years. The proof was that when some of the relationship difficulties were unraveled, he was able to enter into a Holy Communion relationship with God and man. The constructive implication of this is that one of the remote ways of preparation for the Holy Communion is in the experience of feeding which we give our babies. It teaches the human-life language of love without which the divine love cannot be received. Because we have fallen into an unrelated way of thinking in this day of specialization, we may ask how a mother's feeding of her baby contributes to the baby's future capacity to enter into Holy Communion. For the Christian, all things are related and nothing that has true meaning is irrelevant. The truth about God must contain the truth about man; and the truth about man must prepare for and ask for the truth about God. We are not surprised, therefore, when we discover that communion between mother and child, centering in the child's need for food, has meaning and value for all human relations, especially the ultimate one, the relation to God.

Someone has said that this age has rediscovered the meaning and power of love. Important as this insight is, it still does not meet our need, as we shall see. What we need is the *love* that has the power to save. Many of us are reading books and articles on how to raise our children. These tell us again and again that all we need to do is to love our children, and they will be all right. We have discovered that our love does not produce such easy and simple success. Something obviously is wrong, but not with the belief in love, providing we understand concretely what we mean by love. The book is right. As a matter of fact, the experts are more right than they know.

If I could love my child with the kind of love he needs, in the degree to which he needs it, he would be prepared as perfectly as a man could prepare him for real meeting between God and man. To that extent, at least, my love would have saving effect. I want to love him perfectly because I erroneously think *I* must meet his every need as if I were God, and I cannot love him perfectly because I am not God. I see my child's desperate need of love. I can see it in his fears, and in his pathetic joy. I can see it in his frustrations and in his longings. I can see it in his waking and in his sleeping. My heart aches, because in my heart is a desire for him to be loved with the love he needs. But what actually happens? I find that sometimes I do not give him even perfect human love, much less the divine love, that all too often I am unjust and cruel; and at those times he tells me that I do not like him. And yet I do love him and want him to be strengthened and blessed by my love. This is my predicament, and I am sure it is yours, too. We see the need; we long to meet the need. We try to meet our child's need of love, but we not only fail to love him that well, we find ourselves at times giving him the very opposite of what he needs.

What is wrong? There are two aspects of our failure as parents: first, we are tempted to usurp God's place in our child's life by trying to satisfy his need for the divine love with our human love; and second, our human parental love is limited by our sin. Let us look at the situation that reveals our dilemma. The difficulty is that my child—your child—*needs love most when he is most unlovable.* But what does he receive? His unlovableness brings out our unlovableness. Our unlovableness becomes for him our unlovingness so that he not only does not get the love that he needs, but he gets an unlovingness that he does not need.

·87·

In order to do justice to the meaning of the Gospel, I want to make clear what I mean by unlovableness. I do not mean mere personal unattractiveness. By unlovableness I mean that fundamental antagonism to love that is the deepest meaning of sin. And the antagonism is not merely a hostility to human love but (more unlovable still) to the perfect love of God.

If I were to try to love my child to the degree to which he needs to be loved, his unlovableness would force me to a final and ultimate giving of love that is infinitely beyond my ability to give. This is my temptation, to be the Christ, to repeat the once and for all sacrifice. No man is secure enough in his own being to face and meet the unlovable's deepest need for love. Not only would I lose my life, but as a being I would be destroyed. I can point to a portrayal of the love that has the power to love as we cannot and of what happens to that love. The only place we can see love that has the power to love the unlovable in his moment of greatest unlovableness is the love that we see on the Cross. And what do we see there? We see love suffering. It is more than just the suffering of a dying man; pure love is suffering the awful burden and pain of the unlovable. It is loving to the uttermost, and for a moment following the suffering, the agony of loving the unlovable brings extinction—death. Love dies in the process of swallowing up, absorbing, taking unto itself that which is its opposite—unlovableness. This is the kind of demand that unlovableness makes of love. This is why we, with our broken human love, are unable to love our children to the degree to which our children need to be loved. Their need for love is a demand for perfect love; and not only can I not meet that demand, but I hate and rebel against it. And it has become no less true, as we saw earlier, that I also want to meet my child's demand for love. Just as trust must contend against mistrust, so love must contend against hate. The final struggle between them took place on the Cross. The Resurrection is the victory of the love of Christ on the other side of his struggle with the hate of men. The Holy Spirit is the Giver of the love that is victorious. It is God's will that you and I should receive this gift for our struggles.

Human love, therefore, is unequal to the demands of unlovableness. We can become heroic and increase in self-giving altruistic capacities; but, like a rubber band, the more we move away from our egocentric pole, the stronger is the pull to our natural center. "Let him that thinketh he stands take heed lest he fall." The moment I become conscious of how generously I love, in that moment my "love" separates me from the rest of you. The moment I begin to be pleased with my humility, it becomes pride. Little wonder is it that in spite of our best efforts, we are alienated, lonely, and looking for someone who can extricate us from our predicament, someone with whom we can be at one, and through whom we can find at-oneness with all. Human love alone cannot break down the barriers of separation of person from person, life from life as they need to be broken down. And so man, in his walk through life, cries aloud for one with whom he can be at one. This is a part of the life of every family—this is a part of the life of every husband and wife—this is a part of the life of every human relationship, of whatever kind.

A group of parents had voluntarily formed themselves into a study group as a result of instruction they had received for the baptism of their children. One evening they came to the insight we have been discussing, namely, the recognition of the full nature of the child's need for love and of the inability of their own love to meet that need. When the meaning of the truth struck them, several members of the group expressed themselves in ways that revealed that they felt caught in a hopeless dilemma. Their comments had the force of St. Paul's words when similarly confronted: "O wretched man that I am, who shall deliver me from the body of this death."

When they returned the following week and were assembling for a continuation of the discussion, one of them said, "You know, we got along better this week than ever before." To which another couple replied, "You did? Isn't that strange; so did we!" One by one they gave their witness that the past week had been happier. This was surprising because each had expected the opposite result. Intrigued, they began to inquire about the cause of the unexpected result. The one reason for the improvement in their relations was, they discovered, the fact that for the first time in their lives they had become aware of and had accepted some of the meaning of the truth that they were sinful, separated, finite beings and were unable, therefore, to love perfectly and completely. They had not only been perfectionists, they had been godless perfectionists. They had assumed that they should and could do all that was needed, and their inability to do so aroused in them an anxiety that in the end produced in their families tension rather than relaxation, irritability rather than peace, resentment rather than love.

It is not always understood that these unhappy conditions are the result of "bad" theology. The theology is bad in that the previous way of life of these people was based on the assumption, which became their "faith," that man can and must do anything—even love another redemptively. This means that there is no need for God except as a symbol of man's ability.

After that moment of insight, when they saw that the child needs love most when he is most unlovable, and that their love was not equal to the demand, they began to possess a Christian theology. Their concept of man (what theologians speak of as the doctrine of man) became one that accepted the capacity of man to love, and to conceive even of perfect human love, but which recognized his incapacity to love perfectly, and much less to do what only God's love can do, love redemptively. So the young parents in the group, having accepted the sinful imperfections of their love, to some extent gave up trying to do the impossible, namely, to do the work of the perfect love of God.

Please note that the young parents did not give up trying! Instead of trying to do the impossible, they were ready to be content to try, humbly, to accept their need of help. It is tragic when people give up trying, but it is wonderful when they give up trying to do the impossible. The first sign of change was a greater revelation of relationship. A new spirit indwelt the families. This was their first step in the redemptive process. They soon realized, however, that this more realistic belief about themselves and man was not possible to accept without leading to defeatism or another belief. They saw this in terms of their children's persistent need for a love that they, the parents, could not give. The situation needed some source of love that could meet this "deep" need for love; otherwise, as they said, it was a cruel situation. Their understanding of man's need, thus, asked for a belief in God.

The Spirit that had led them this far in their spiritual

pilgrimage made known to them that God is revealed in Jesus Christ; and the Scripture, the source book of that revelation, was opened to them by the Church, whose business it is through the Spirit to make Him known to all men. They read the Gospels and saw there the Person who had the power to heal person-hurts. Then they saw the Cross as the revelation of the love that has the power to save the unlovable. That such love once dwelt among men is wonderful, but where is it now? Can it be ours? If so, how? Then they discovered St. Paul's teaching which made known to them that *agape*—God's love—is a gift given by the Holy Spirit.

What does this mean? they asked. The answer slowly emerged out of their study. First, they recognized that their own little group was characterized by a spirit. Then they remembered their experience of school spirit and realized that the spirit of a school creates the group and is known in the group that it creates. The school spirit lives in relation. It is not in the "I" of this person or that, but between the "I" and the "Thou." Only through entering into relation can man find and live in the spirit. The young couples had already experienced this, and its meaning was partially available to them. Their common need and inquiry into that need had formed them into a fellowship through which a new spirit of understanding and love possessed them. This spirit would not have come to them if they had dwelt apart in isolation. Only as they allowed the Spirit to draw them into relation did the Spirit come to them. On the basis of this experience they began to understand the New Testament teaching about the Holy Spirit. They came to see that working upon them through their needs, through the Church, through the sacrament of baptism, through their relationship with their minister, the Holy Spirit drew them into a fellowship in which they sensed a new presence and power in their lives.

Their first experience of these things came through their small group, but they realized as time passed that their little "church" had served its purpose and must go They recognized, however, their continuing need of the Spirit, and so they sought Him in the group of His own creation—the Church. God gives the gift of His power to those who through the Spirit are united with one another in Him. Wherever the Spirit of God is, there you find the love of God; and where people are open to the Spirit of·God, you have a people who are the means of making this uncommon and saving love available to men. So it is that God has encounter with men in and through his people. We cannot experience His love solely by reading about it; we cannot experience His love apart from encounter with Him. And so He first revealed His love to men in His Incarnate Son living in person-to-person relationship. Now, we may experience His love through person-to-person encounter with those who are born into the relationship of His Spirit.

This has been the experience of countless Christians through the centuries: first there is the Spirit-filled Church which should draw people back to it again and again; second there is the Christ, whom the Church, through the Spirit, holds before men; and third through Him is the Father known. Christianity is Trinitarian. We are sent to a suffering people who suffer because they have not found at-oneness in *the* love that has power to reconcile and reunite a man to himself and his fellows. Our business as the Church is the business for which God brought her into being, namely, to be the relationship through which men may experience, at least partially, the love of God that reconciles us to Himself and to one another. Again, this is the Good News.

Through the centuries the commonly agreed purpose of the Christian fellowship living in the world is to witness to the love of God and to be the personal instruments of His love. If someone should come and ask "Where shall I find and experience the love of God?", we can only direct him to the people of God in whom His Spirit dwells. "The Holy Ghost Himself is Love," wrote Gregory in one of his homilies. And in the

dusty *Sentences* of Peter Lombard, Chapter I is en-
titled "The Holy Spirit Is the Love by Which We
Love God and the Neighbor." The meaning of this
passage is that love in the highest sense comes from
God and only as we have His gift of love can we have
the power and ability to meet the terrible demand to
love and the demand for love.

My faith is, therefore, that God uses my power of
love, limited and sinful though it is, to prepare my child
for the experience of His reconciling and fulfilling love.
So real is this that I believe that God is able to transcend the limitations of my love and that my child may
experience more than my love for him. Out of these
encounters, this language of relationship, he will ac-
cumulate meanings that will make available to him
some day the fuller meaning of God's great love for
him; and release through his limited power of loving
others, God's saving love for them. In this way, the
Church's language of relationship provides the experiences that produce the meanings necessary for understanding the great words and concepts of our faith.

The final and ultimate necessity for the gift of love
is that the love relationship is an indispensable precon-
dition for worship. The first expression of Christian
prayer is adoration. Without love, we cannot worship.
Since worship is primarily a relationship of expressed
love, our promise means that we will pray that God's

love will help us to love our children so that they will be prepared to respond to the love of God. The keeping of this promise is not easy as we have seen, and the experience of love not always serene and fulfilling; but through all the various experiences there needs to emerge a deep trust and sense of relationship and sense of the Spirit. We need the presence of Another indwelling us to whom, more and more, we recognize that we belong; to whom, more and more, we want to give ourselves; and from whom, more and more, we want to take to others the same gift of deep confidence and love. This is what it means to be His Church and to engage in what is supposed to be her most characteristic activity, worship, from which comes the preserving and transforming power to do His reconciling work.

How wonderful that the Church created by God to do His gracious work is made up of men, even ourselves! Though we are honored by being made a means of redemption, we yet are always in need of redemption. The full blessing of the Spirit is to be one for whom God Incarnate died; to be one who lives for others; to be forgiven *and* forgiving; to be reconciled *and* reconciling; to be loved *and* loving.

CHAPTER SEVEN

GOD'S ACCEPTANCE
AND OURS

THE CHILD'S next need is the need for acceptance, and acceptance is an expression of love. Every child, every person needs to be accepted as an individual in his own right. We give acceptance when we accept the fact of each other's existence and the difference that the existence of others makes to us and to our way of living. For example, I accept my child when I accept the fact of his existence and the welcome and unwelcome differences in my life that his presence causes. Now that he is here, for example, we cannot drop the dishes in the sink and run off to the movies! By "unwelcome" differences I mean that in some respects the presence of another, even our own child, gets in our way, causes fatigue, makes demands difficult to meet, causes deprivation of freedom and enjoyment; and unless we can at least be prepared to accept that in these respects it is not easy to accept a child or another person, the chances are good that he will feel unwelcome. Some people, however, are quite disturbed by the suggestion that they do not completely love their children, or that any of the differences the children make in their way of living are unwelcome. They prefer to believe that it is all gain and are unable to accept that with every gain there is always pain.

A young mother was in great distress because she was afraid that she might do harm to her new baby and found it increasingly difficult, therefore, to take care of him. Both she and her husband had planned for and welcomed his birth. Consequently, she could not understand why now she should want to hurt him. The explanation of the mother's situation illustrates the point that is being made. For seven years she had traveled with her husband while waiting for their first baby. In spite of their disappointment at not having a family, they both had had a happy time traveling together. When their baby finally came, they were overjoyed; but the fact of his existence meant that she could no longer be with her husband. Although she unquestionably wanted and loved the baby, she missed being with her husband and unconsciously resented the baby because he was the reason she had to stay at home. Her feelings about him were mixed. She could accept her positive feelings about him, but not the negative ones.

Many of us, like this mother, erroneously think that if we have any antagonistic feelings about another person, it must mean that there is something wrong with us or that we do not really love the other regardless of how much evidence there may be that we do. Not being able to accept the unwelcome difference her child made in her life, she pretended that that kind of difference did not exist. That is like pretending that there is no prowler in our house when there is. It leaves him free to do all kinds of harm. In the mother's case, the unaccepted and undealt with resentment came out through an unconscious process in the form of a desire to injure (in reality to get rid of) her baby. After a time, she was helped to accept both feelings—to accept the unwelcome as well as the welcome differences her child made—and she lost her fear that she would hurt him.

Not everyone has the problem of acceptance in such a dramatic form, but everyone has it in some form. Actually, we cannot completely accept anyone, although either the literature on the subject of acceptance or the way people read and understand it suggests that acceptance is something that one can give another at will. Underlying this kind of thinking is a very naive concept of man that leaves us unprepared both for all the good we cannot do and for all the evil we can so easily do. To command or suggest to another the obligation of perfect acceptance is to lay an intolerable and destructive burden upon him. The most accepting person both accepts and rejects his child and other people. The question is not whether I do or do not accept but rather what is the proportion of acceptance and rejection in my relationships with others.

When I accept my child, therefore, I can only say that predominantly I am glad that he is. This is my acceptance of him; and because he lives in relation to my gladness mixed with my irritation, hostility, anxiety, and other feelings, he picks up my most characteristic attitude toward him as his attitude toward himself. Thus as I predominantly accept him, he is helped to accept himself. It is good to have happy, friendly feelings toward one's self, to have affirmative feelings about one's being in spite of some negative feelings. Anyone who works with people knows how common it is for men and women to have predominantly disparaging feelings toward themselves. They cannot believe in themselves or that other men or even God accept them. They feel this way because it is the way the important people in their lives have felt about them.

Thus, I need to accept my child in order that he may accept himself—he needs to become a part of an accepting community. But this is not the end of the process. He needs all this acceptance in order that he may become the kind of person who can accept others, who also need acceptance; and only the self-accepting can accept others.

It is difficult to find a self-rejecting person who does much in the way of accepting others. As has been indicated, acceptance is not easy; and one reason why it is not is that every person demands acceptance of us and we of him. This demand for acceptance is implicit in every relation; and because it makes more of a demand on me than I wish, I resent it. Because I was not completely accepted, I am not sufficiently self-accepting to be able to accept others as they need to be. Here is another vicious circle that needs to be broken by the power of some person who is secure enough to meet the demand for acceptance. We know that no man can meet this demand; but Christ, the God-man did.

Our understanding of our need of acceptance is now taking on a new meaning. At first it seemed wholly psychological, but now it seems religious and theological. It has to do with the very nature of our being. When I have a strong sense of the acceptance of someone who is important to me, I have a security that makes it possible for me to face the full truth about myself (what I am, what I can do) and say, "This is I." I do not have to pretend to be what I am not. I do not have to hide my inadequacies or build up my capacities unrealistically as many people have to do. When we pretend to be what we are not, it is a good sign that we feel vulnerable; and we feel vulnerable because we do not have the security that comes from a sense of acceptance. Likewise, because of this same security, I can more nearly accept the unacceptable truths about myself—the things about myself that I do not like. For instance, I can get down on my knees and say that I am a sinner and really mean it. Perhaps this is why the Church puts the General Confession in the context of worship, a context in which we experience a relationship that gives us greatest security. One cannot really surrender one's pretenses and defenses when he is insecure and vulnerable. Only when we are secure and have the assurance of acceptance dare we be honest about what we are and are not. A relationship of security does not solve our problems but it frees us from anxiety about ourselves and helps us see and use our resources that are necessary if we are to deal constructively with our problems.

Acceptance is important, especially when we think of it in terms of the acceptance that comes from God; indeed, this is what justification by faith means according to the definition of Calvin, who many years before the psychological age said that justification by faith is God's acceptance of us in Christ. Here is the real Source of acceptance. Here is the One who makes it possible for me to accept more fully the truth about myself.

This same sense of personal security born of acceptance makes me able to help my neighbor, to accept him and his demand for acceptance. Now I can really understand him in the sense of standing under him. When does a man need someone to stand under him? When he is shaky. When does a man need understanding? When he is feeling misunderstood and is the hardest to understand. When does a man need acceptance? When he is feeling unacceptable. And I cannot give him the acceptance he needs because of my own needs. We all need acceptance; and although God created the Church to meet this need, we have to admit that when a person is most vulnerable he often receives the least acceptance from us.

How easily we forget that God shows His love for us in that "while we were yet sinners Christ died for us."[1] He accepts us and creates us into a reconciling fellowship for the express purpose of providing acceptance for the unacceptable. How then can we justify the rejection, ridicule, scorn which we so easily give those who have offended by thought, word, or deed? We exist in the name of Christ not to exclude the lost and to include the righteous, but to seek out and include the lost and count ourselves as outsiders except as we seek to bring others in. One young man learned a profound lesson about the nature of the Church. He had lost his faith as a result of a long and involved intellectual and religious pilgrimage and, as a result of his agnosticism, was doing and saying many things that were hurting some of the people who loved him. An elderly pastor tried to reach and help him in several ways, but without much success. Finally he said to the young man: "I have done everything I can think of to help you to a

[1] Rom. 5:8.

faith by which you can live. Having failed, I can only believe for you—I shall believe for you until you can believe for yourself." In time the young man found again a faith that sustained him, but the power of another's faith held him during the interim.

Some years ago I served in a consultative capacity to what was then called the Church Mission of Help (now the Youth Consultation Service), an organization that sought to help unmarried mothers. Many young girls were helped, but a snag was sometimes struck when the time came to help the girl to find a place in the life of a parish. If and when the facts about the girl came out, she occasionally found herself unwanted. Are we a society of the forgiven and the forgiving?

Our conclusion thus far is that acceptance is not easy. It calls for a power that we sooner or later recognize is not in us.

The commandment for acceptance is not one we can keep. On the other hand, the situation is not as bad as it seems. The ultimate realization of the relationship that we are talking about is the Kingdom of God. If the Kingdom of God means anything at all, if the Kingdom of God *is* the Kingdom of God, it at the least means a relationship in which we know the acceptance of God. And the Kingdom of God is not something that you and I have to build. After all, it is the Kingdom *of* God, and this means the kingdom of His creation and of which He is the sole sovereign. He is the answer to our need for acceptance. From Him comes the acceptance that makes it possible to become a fellowship of acceptance through which He meets our needs.

The answer to our need for a really accepting acceptance is to be found in God's action in our behalf. Baptism may, therefore, be regarded as the sacrament of God's acceptance of us. In baptism we come to a point in the service where the minister says, "Name this child," and immediately the Church baptizes him and says, "John Joseph, I baptize thee in the Name of the Father, and of the Son, and of the Holy Ghost."

What are we doing here? We are doing many things, but among them we are, in the first place, identifying this child as this particular child of God; for by this name shall he be known forever, and by this name shall he be distinguished from every other child of God. This is the Church's verbal and ceremonial acceptance of him as an individual in his own right, and the quality of that individuality has the quality of being a child of God. We said, on the other hand, that in order for an individual to become a person, he needs to be a part of a structure of relationship. Without that he can not be and will die.

Next in the baptismal service come these words: "We receive this child into the congregation of Christ's flock." This is the act of the Christian community (the new order of redeemed personal relations) receiving this child into its structural relationship in order that that which is ritually affirmed may begin to take place in the life of the child and in the relationship into which he is reborn. The purpose of baptism is that the child shall become what he is (child of God) in contrast to the human tendency of pretending to be what one is not.

If we are secure in a relationship that makes clear that we are persons of distinction, we do not find it necessary to pretend to be what we are not. It is the function of the Church to know us as children of God so that we may become such and not have to pretend to be an unreal someone in order to find significance. In this way the child acquires his identity and comes into his inheritance. Otherwise, there would be no way for him to know his identity or inheritance. The words "We receive this child into the congregation of Christ's Church," refer to the subsequent and continuing action of God through the Church following the rite of baptism.

What we are to become, we have said, depends on how we have been known. We have identified this as a principle that underlies the meaning of baptism and of the Church as a redemptive community. I wonder if we realize how true this principle is. When a friend of mine, in middle life, discovered great enjoyment in creative manual activity of all kinds, he wondered how it happened that he had lived so long under the belief that he was lacking in manual dexterity and skill. He remembered, finally, that when he was a child he was told, and heard his parents comment to others, that he could not do anything with his hands, that his "fingers were all thumbs." Their conception of him became his conception of himself. They accepted him as clumsy, and he accepted himself as such.

Here is a negative illustration of a principle the Church is supposed to embody positively. We are to see, know, and accept the child as the child of God in order that he may become one. This is the intention of baptism, and baptism is not for the child alone but for the whole baptismal fellowship. One practical implication of this insight is that when the rite is administered, the whole congregation should be present.

We need to pursue further how, through God's acceptance of us, we can accept the newly baptized so that they will come to know themselves as children of God and be able to enter into the fullness of that relationship. Elsewhere in the service of baptism, the Church makes some promises on behalf of the child, and among them is the promise to teach the child the Creed. What do we promise to do? I am sure we will all agree, when we stop to think about it, that we promise to do a great deal more than merely to teach the child the verbal formulas known as either the Nicene or the Apostles' Creed. We may well suspect, following our discussion in the previous chapter, that somehow we ought to employ the language of relationship, but how can the meanings of the Creed be approached through relationship? In the first four words of the Creed are the two most important words that the human being uses: the word I by which he identifies himself, and the word God (for which we can substitute the word "Thou" because it refers to God and our neighbor as well).

Each of us brings his own meanings to the use of these two words, meanings that he has learned in his relationship with the important people in his life. One man brings such egocentric meanings to them that we have to brace ourselves against him lest he suck us into his egocentric way of life. God becomes a minor satellite moving vaguely on the outer edge of his universe. Consequently, he uses the word "Thou" with the same self-centered meaning with which he uses the word "I." The fact that he says the Creed once a week may have only contradictory rather than saving meaning.

Here is another person who brings more positive meanings to his use of the important words. The effect of his presence is to bring out, encourage, and strengthen the trust and capabilities of those around him. He brings to human encounter an outgoing, helpful, accepting, and self-disciplined relationship. We realize that this person's center is outside himself. He is a religious man.

What is the source of the meanings we bring to our use of these two most important words? As Martin Buber has helped us to see, they grow out of our experiences in relation to our most important "Thou's," namely, our parents, our teachers, and others who have had a determinative influence on our lives.[2] They were our "Thou's" in relation to our "I," and we were their "Thou" in relation to their "I."

The role of the "Thou" is to reveal the meaning of existence to the "I" who confronts him. The role of the parent is to reveal the meaning of existence to his child, the teacher to his pupil, the preacher to his hearer, and the pastor to his parishioner. Likewise, the child, the pupil, the hearer, the parishioner is a "Thou" in relation to his parent, his teacher, his preacher, and his pastor, and has *also* the responsibility of revealing the meaning of existence to them. Indeed, only an uncomprehending parent or teacher fails to realize that he learns from his children and his pupils much that he could not possibly learn otherwise.

It should be noticed that in saying that the role of the "Thou" is to *reveal*, we are using a technical word. "Reveal" is a theological word. "Revelation" is pre-emi-

[2] Martin Buber, *I and Thou*. (Edinburgh, T. and T. Clark, 1944.)

nently the function of the "Eternal Thou"; *God* reveals. But because we are made in His image and we possess some of His image, we retain the capacity to reveal. Revelation by its very nature is personal. Therefore, what is implied here is a definition of Christian education. Christian education must be personal; it must take place in a personal encounter *and, only secondarily, is it transmissive.* On the other hand, Christian education is responsible for the continued recital of God's saving acts and of the transmission of the subject matter of the historical faith and life of the Christian community. The content of our faith was born of God's action and man's response—a divine-human encounter. It is possible, however, to reduce it to subject matter and substitute the transmission of subject matter for the encounter, with the assumption that it will accomplish the same purpose (although it cannot, it never has, and it never will). Actually, the relations of encounter and transmission are complementary. Both are needed. The Church as a "tradition-bearing community" contains both poles and does not want to subordinate one to the other. When the content of the tradition is lost, the meaning of the encounter is lost, and in the end even encounter itself. And when encounter is lost, tradition becomes idolatrous and sterile. Both are necessary to the faith community, and both are dangerous and meaningless if separated. And Christian teaching must depend upon both.

The content of the Christian faith is the fruit of the action of the "Eternal Thou" in and through the "Thou" of Jesus of Nazareth in personal encounter with men. This encounter has content, and it can be identified, formulated, and interpreted. As such, however, it is only a part of the truth. Separated from the relationship out of which it came, it is without saving power. As unrelated content, it is in danger of becoming a substitute for the relationship, and therefore, an idol. We are not saved by knowledge alone, and yet without content a relationship can become formless, purposeless, and destructive. Only as my life is "hid with Christ in God"[3] can my knowing have its full meaning.

The conception of Christian education that grows out of our thought thus far is one which recognizes that out of the experience in relationship the person brings meaning to his use of the two most important words "I" and "Thou" that will help him choose to be in relation to God and others in spite of the meanings in him that will drive him to choose against man and God.

One indispensable doorway to the meaning of the

[3] Col. 3:3.

creed and God's action for me is through the meaning I bring to the first four words "I believe in God." What kind of meanings do I bring? If basic trust is present in me, then when I say "I" and "Thou," much that is represented by the word *believe* is implicit in my affirmation. I am now prepared to move from basic trust, as I have known it in my human relationship, to faith in Him who is the ground and source of my being. In so doing, I bring my human relations into that larger faith which their final undependability demands. Then the meanings of "I" in relation to "Thou" (on whatever level of understanding, human or divine) are determinative for all meaning. Therefore, the individual's understanding of God's saving acts as stated in the creed is restricted or enhanced by these fundamental "I-Thou" meanings.

This may give us a clue to what we mean when we promise to teach the child the creed. Among other things, the Church promises to assume responsibility for the contributions of all relationships to the meanings that this child will bring to his use of these two most important words. In other words, we make a promise to teach through a relationship of acceptance, as well as by words, so that the verbal formulas of faith will have meanings to complete the meanings the child brings out of his life. This is a more appropriate responsibility for the Church to assume than one of just teaching words by rote, since it partakes of the very nature of the Church itself.

If the child through the experience of acceptance can bring the right meaning of trust to his use of these two most important words, then all that the creed affirms about what God has done in relation to human need will become more available to him. Unless we help him at this level, we will often find that the words about our Christian faith may not make available to him the saving effects of the fact that God accepts him. In fact, they become obstacles to their availability. Have you not known people who said that the Apostles' Creed left them cold?

From time to time in our discussion we have observed that we cannot accept our children to the extent to which they need to be accepted because our capacity for acceptance is limited by our need to reject one another. The "good news" of the Gospel is that God in Christ accepts us and therefore releases in us a power of acceptance that is not ours by nature. But how do we experience His acceptance?

To know ourselves to be His, regardless of what we are or have done. How we would love to have this kind of acceptance! This is a part of that need I was talking about, the need to be at one with someone and to have someone at one with us. How we should love that, but how is God to express it? How can we possibly experience this acceptance? We cannot experience it by reading about it. We can read the Bible, the Gospel story, we can see it portrayed in the Book of Common Prayer, we can have someone tell us about it, but still that is not the experience we want.

We can experience love and acceptance through personal encounter only. How, then, does God effect the personal encounter that communicates His power of acceptance? There is only one way, the way He has provided. In the first place, He visited His people historically and in incarnate personal encounter revealed Himself to us. We know Him to be the Christ, our Lord, and we would have constant companionship with Him. But we, in this generation, cannot live with Him as He was in His generation. We can know the historic Jesus only through reading about Him and through our power of imaginative identification. To be sure, this is a resource, but it is not the fellowship that God intends us to have.

Thank God, we are offered even more than this. Our Lord said that it was expedient for us that He go away. He said that in His place He would send us a Comforter, and that when He came, He (the Spirit) would lead us into all truth. The coming of the Holy Spirit brought into being the new creation, the new relationship between God and man, His instrument in History—the Church. This is a relationship of men caught up into a relationship with God, created by God in order that He may enter into saving encounter with men, a means by which men may experience His gifts of acceptance (forgiveness and reconciliation) and love. This means that His acceptance of us is communicated by His Spirit in and through our acceptance of each other. My task of faith as a parent or teacher is to be open to God in order that He may express His acceptance of my child in and through my limited and broken ability to accept him. This would seem to limit God's acceptance, except that He is able to transcend our limitation and do in and through us what we of ourselves are completely incapable of doing. God can act in any way He wants, but He wants to act through us and He wants us to act in response to Him. We believe that His Spirit can re-create us. He must be able, therefore, to re-create our power of acceptance.

Our faith is not in ourselves and in what we can do, but in God and in what He can do in and through us. We are His new creation called to the task of continuing in our generation His reconciling work through the gift of acceptance with men who feel so very unacceptable. Finally, I want to make clear that the acceptance of God, *pointed to* through human acceptance, exceeds anything that human acceptance can ever convey. But it can only be pointed to, seen, and responded to by faith.

CHAPTER EIGHT

GOD'S DISCIPLINE
AND OURS

THE THIRD NEED of the individual is the need for discipline. Having discussed the child's need for love and acceptance, we come now to his need for discipline. Contrary to what we may first think about it, discipline is related to love and acceptance. An understanding of our need for discipline is necessary not only for a more complete understanding of the role of the other two needs but for a more complete understanding of God's action as well.

When anyone mentions discipline, most of us think of punishment for misbehavior. But by discipline we mean more than concern for the principle and methods of punishment. Instead, it may be thought of as a structure for existence within which a child may grow up. It should be *protective* because the child can do nothing for himself at first; it should provide *guidance* because he has so much to learn; and it should be *permissive* because he needs freedom to choose, even to choose wrong!

Our children need this kind of relationship because they are strangers in a strange life. They do not know themselves because they do not know anyone else. They are dropped like tiny mites into the mighty onrushing stream of life that can so easily overwhelm and destroy them. We have to protect them against their own weakness and the terrible strength of a vast, powerful, impersonal culture. One of our great and enduring fears is the fear of being lost in the flood of life; "lost in the crowd." Out of this relation between the individual and the complexity and immensity of life are born the deep anxieties and feelings of loneliness. For this reason, as we have seen, our children need relationships of acceptance and love. The first sense awakened in them as a result of their experience of these is a sense of trust. A child needs this trust in order to come into his next inheritance, a sense of autonomy. There begins in the second year a struggle in the child between being an autonomous creature and being a dependent one. As a result of this struggle, he begins to be able to identify himself as a person in relation to other persons, and, as we saw earlier, his achievement of personhood is dependent upon the "being" of his significant people being persons. We find it more difficult to accept, however, that the acquisition of autonomous personhood is accomplished only by struggle and resistance. In the inevitable resistance between parent and child, the child may become a person. Whether or not he does depends in large part upon what the parent can bring to the encounter in the way of love and stability. Such an insight makes it possible to meet the rebelliousness of two-year-olds with more acceptance. We now see its purpose.

The need of the individual for a protective, guiding, and permissive relationship in which to live is represented by the symbol of the play pen. The play pen has two functions: one, to keep the child in; the other, to keep the world out. The boundaries of the play pen set up for the child limitations beyond which he may not go and which provide for him an early experience of the restraint of *authority*. At the same time he is allowed, within these boundaries, an experience of *freedom* to do pretty much as he pleases. It should be noted that his experiences of authority and freedom come from the same source. If our experiences of authority and freedom could be kept mutually harmonious, most of our problems would not exist. We realize, however, that we can have no such utopian expectation. As the child grows up and acquires from his relationship a sense of basic trust, he begins to achieve a sense of autonomy. This dawning sense of independence runs into conflict with the autonomy of others, especially with parents and others who have the authority over him, whose authority he needs, and which he both accepts and resents. As for his experience in the play pen, it should be noted that there are only a few idyllic days in which he is happy in it. In a short time he begins to kick angrily at the bars of restraint and seeks to expand limitlessly his freedom. And he will be slow to stop this kind of behavior when he is let out of the pen. To some degree, we all continue through the whole of our life our rebellions against authority.

Our immature attitudes toward authority are well known. Intellectually we are more ready to accept authority as good for us. Were it not for authority, life would become unbearably chaotic. Emotionally we are more apt to resent authority and want as much freedom as possible. Like the Sheriff of Nottingham, we want what we want when we want it. The truth is that our attitudes toward authority are mixed, but there is a tendency either to fail to recognize or to evade the hostility that our experience with authority arouses. Some of us remember painful conflicts with our parents' exercise of authority and may be aware of the hostility that we feel toward them along with the love we have for them. Our attitudes toward our teachers and traffic policemen are well-known. Humor often expresses hostility toward those in authority who are made the object of the joke.

The question we now need to face is: If our attitudes toward this kind of authority are hostile, what must be the attitude of man without any resource other than himself toward the eternal and holy God, under whose righteous law we are judged and from whom there is no possible escape?

Nietzsche describes the attitude very well in *Thus Spake Zarathustra*. In one episode the ugliest man kills the beautiful god. When he is asked why he killed the beautiful god, he replies, "He had to die." Yes, he had to die; the beautiful god is intolerable to the ugly man. He could not change his ugliness to beauty, and he could not change the beautiful god into an ugly one. Thus, he could only kill the beautiful god. Our situation is very much like this. Our God is beautiful, with the beauty of holiness; our God is altogether holy, pure, and righteous. We are drawn into His presence by the attraction of His loveliness and by our desire and need for Him; but when we are confronted by His holiness, we know ourselves for what we are. The contrast is such that we say with Peter, "Depart from me, O Lord, for I am a sinful man." This is the only conviction that we can have in the face of such holiness and absolute righteousness. Furthermore, we not only resent that He is but also the absolute demand that He makes of us. Not only is His holiness unbearable, but so also is His holy law because we can neither *be* like Him nor *do* His bidding.

I wonder if we have due respect for the demand that religion makes upon us. Religion calls upon us to worship God. What is worship? Worship is adoring, self-surrender; and, as we have seen, it is possible only in a relationship of love. How can you adoringly surrender yourself to One who is intolerable to you and whom you hate because He demands perfect love and holiness of you?

Is it to be wondered that many people find it impossible to go to church? It is not just that they are careless or that church is meaningless, but that they dare not go to church where they will be confronted by Him and His demands. Or, as Mark Twain put it: "It's not what I don't understand in the Bible that bothers me, but what I understand all too well."

Neither is it to be wondered that, among those who go to church, there are those for whom real worship is impossible because worship requires a relationship of love and trust that our feelings of resentment obstruct, unless somehow our feelings can be accepted as a part of the worship. And, unfortunately, Christian nurture has not helped us with this problem. Many of us have the idea that regardless of how we feel, we have to be polite to God and say only nice things to Him. In contrast, any faith we have in Him ought to include a trust that He not only knows how we really feel about Him—that we both love and hate Him—but that He can take it. In our homes, when our children rebel against our authority and express their resentment against us, even to the extent of saying that they want to kill us, we are not always able to accept these hostile expressions. Yet, occasionally, we understand them and are able to permit them to express their feelings, within reasonable limits. Would not Our Lord say to us then, "If you, being evil, know how to give even imperfectly the good gifts" of acceptance to your children in their moments of hostility and unlovableness, "**How** much more will not your heavenly Father . . ." **He** knows, understands, and wants to help us; but **He also** wants us to be honest with Him because no relationship is possible that is not honest.

Here we are confronted by the Holy God, who makes the intolerable demand of perfect obedience of us. We cannot meet this, and therefore resent the demand. We resent the judgment and the death sentence of the holy law. If we could only get rid of God. We cannot change His nature, and we cannot change ours. What can we do? If He lives, I die; if . . . if He dies, then I will live! This is the "ugliest man in relation to the beautiful God" solution.

Now we can begin to see the differences between the Nietzsche story and the Christian story. In the Nietzsche story, the beautiful god is the victim of the ugliest man's initiative. In the Christian story, God is not the passive but the active victim. He is the Initiator of the whole action. He is the Initiator because, in the first place, He is the One who understands the nature of man's need. He comes as a person into the broken order of personal relations to live with men in a face-to-face, person-to-person relationship. And through this process, beginning with this personal, historical encounter and continuing through the coming of the Holy Spirit, He brings into being the new order of redeemed personal relations. But He knew that His perfect love would present us with an intolerable demand, resentment against which would arouse our unlovableness. Is it not strange that even when unlovableness is confronted by the love for which it is seeking, it cannot accept it, but resents it and wants to destroy it? How we need to understand that things are seldom black or white, that we do not either love or hate! Instead, we both love and hate; we both want love and do not want love; we both receive love when it is given to us, and we rebel against love when we experience it. We are like this, and life is like this, and God meets us here in this confused state of being.

When God as man lived with man, it was inevitable that as "beautiful god" He would come into conflict with the ugliest man. Everything about Him was intolerable, even His uncommon love and mercy; and so man killed Him. But He consented to His own death. He, the Absolute One, from whom there was no escape, allowed man the most real freedom, the freedom to rid himself of the hated authority. He chose to be the victim. "No man taketh my life from me; I lay it down of myself." [1] And God is dead! Now that the intolerable

[1] John 10:18.

One is dead, there is none of the expected relief and release; there is now only intolerable loneliness and desolation. The scene is portrayed vividly by the figure of Peter, who, after his denial, "went out and wept bitterly," suffering what he thought to be the ultimate bereavement of final separation. And yet the message of Life reached him while he was in that state: "Go tell His disciples and Peter that He is going before you into Galilee; there you will see him." Another difference between the Nietzsche story and the Christian story appears at this point. In the Nietzsche story the beautiful god stays dead, while in the Christian story the beautiful god comes back. And He comes back and says to us: I am He Whom you feared and hated, but behold, I am alive for evermore. And I love you and there is nothing you can do so far as I am concerned that can destroy my love for you nor the new relationship which I have given you. You may turn your back on me. You may deny me. You may act against me. But so far as I am concerned, you are forever my beloved child. I have died for you, and now I live for you.

And then there is the wonder of discovering that the one we thought we had to fear and hate turns out to be the one, THE ONE, who alone has the power to come and live where we are most alone and separated. Lo, He for whom we have been looking and He whom we feared are the same. By the power of His own love for us, He has met the awful demand of God's intolerable holiness. And the tension between love and justice is resolved forever because now mercy is just and justice is merciful. That is the Good News! The good Christian story! He who comes can reach us in our depths. He is the One with whom we can be at one. He is the beloved, and we know ourselves to be His beloved. This is the great, *good news*. Well, this is what God has done. We know now what St. Paul means when he says that we are saved by His Resurrection. It is only in His coming back that we really know Him. He is Lord because He is God. But I know Him and accept Him as my Lord because He let me kill Him, and then He came back.

Now the question is, what does this drama of redemption mean to us in terms of our present human situation? For unless it means something where we live now, it is a very theoretical sort of gospel and is not really good news. It is only good news if it speaks to us where we are right now.

What does all this mean in relation to the conflicts that grow out of parent-child encounters in which, for the moment, the predominating spirit is one of alienation and hostility? Here is a story that may help. The two persons involved are a Christian mother and her eight-year-old daughter. The daughter had done something that had made her feel alienated from her mother

and for which she felt guilty. Her mother had been trying to help her. Angry and hostile, the child stamped
out of the room and went upstairs. There she found a
new dress that her mother was going to wear to a party
that night. Nearby was a pair of scissors that her mother
had been using. She picked up the scissors and muti-
lated the dress, thereby symbolically and actually injur-
ing her mother. After a while the mother came up to
her room and saw what her daughter had done. She
was heartbroken and threw herself down on the bed
and cried. Pretty soon the little girl came in and walked
slowly up to the bed. "Mother," she whispered anx-
iously. No reply. "Mother—Mother." No reply. "Mother,
Mother, please," again pled the daughter. After a moment the mother asked, "Please what?" "Please take me
back, please take me back," prayed the little girl.

This is the cry of man. Do you hear it? We who are
the Church do not always hear that cry. We sometimes
say that the world is not interested in what we have,
and so we go into our churches and close the doors behind us. The clergy settle down to be chaplains to the
faithful, and the faithful just settle down. Outside those
closed doors go thousands and millions of men and
women who in one way or another cry, "Please take
me back." They do not know that they cry, or for what,
or that the answer lies behind those closed doors. It is
just possible that if we can hear their cry, they may hear

our answer. Ours? No, not our answer, God's—God's answer to them through us, His Church.

We return now to the bedroom where the little girl is asking her mother to take her back. This is all she can do. She can only ask to be restored to the relationship that she broke. There is nothing that she can do to mend the break, reconcile the alienation, or restore herself to the former state of being.

Children experience alienation from their important people and try in various ways to be at one with them again. And have you not noticed how they try ways that the people of God tried through the centuries and which are portrayed in the Old Testament? A little boy will go out and pick up some little thing that is of value to him but of no value to the parent, bring it in to her and say, "Mother, I'm sorry. Here's a present for you." The gift may be a sign of repentance and good will, but it cannot effect atonement. Or the little child will come to the mother and say, "Mother, I'm sorry I was bad; from now on I will be good. I'll never do anything wrong again." And religious people have gone to their God and said, "God, we are sorry that we broke your laws, and from now on we will be perfectly obedient." How pathetic! You know the little child cannot be that good, and if he can, why was he not? Furthermore, present goodness cannot cancel past badness. The little fellow may run upstairs and shut himself in his room and say, "I've been a bad boy, go to my room." Sackcloth and ashes! Self-punishment! The most that one can say for this method is that it may be a sign of true repentance which could receive forgiveness if there is a forgiveness. But there is nothing that the child can do to create the forgiveness. He can only ask that he be taken back. Forgiveness is "beforehand giveness" of self. It can come only from the injured side.

Have we not learned this? Who has not betrayed or hurt another and known that terrifying feeling when it finally dawned on him that what he has done is irrevocable? How we long to find some way of undoing the hurt, and how awful to realize that not only have we found nothing to do but that we never will! We experience the same futility with regard to the possibility of finding something to do that will cover the first act. But there is nothing, nothing, nothing. We can only cry, "Please take me back."

And so, returning to our story again, the mother reached out her arm and drew her daughter to her. This human act has the meaning of atonement; and only the parent, human or divine, can make things right, can effect the atonement. God heard our cry. He took us back. And the mother, herself a child of God, redeemed by Christ, indwelt by His Spirit, is open to His atoning action through her for the child.

We need to be careful at this point to be clear about

the nature of the mother's action. How easy it would have been for the mother to have punished the child vindictively (as we all on occasion have done) and added to the child's offense one of her own that would have further increased their separation from each other and others. And how tempted the mother may have been to forgive heroically and offer her human forgiveness as a substitute for God's forgiveness as if she were God. Had she done this she would have become a barrier to the child's future encounter with and response to God.

Instead, the mother, out of her Christian relationship, responded to the child's need with the forgiveness with which she herself has been forgiven. Because of the forgiveness and reconciliation that we have from God in Christ, the mother's action becomes not only a witness to but also an instrument of God's atoning action. The daughter's experience now has a meaning that will help prepare her for participation in God's atonement. Thus does God work through person to person. Here in this family was the little church that for the moment was responsive to God and effective for Him. Thus the parent-child relationship is more than an analogy of the relationship of man to God; it is one of the means of God's action insofar as He can indwell and act through it, *but it can never be regarded as a substitute for the relationship with God.*

God reconciled the world unto Himself; the mother reconciled the child to herself. So much is clear. There is a danger here that the child will be left to receive her reconciliation as the gift of the parent saying, as it were, "This is what parents are like." Instead, she should be led to say, "This is what Christ has made parents to be." In other words, reconciliation is always the gift of God Who seeks to make this kind of relationship one of the occasions for the accomplishment of His atoning action for this child.

In this way did the mother in our story teach by the language of relationship. And little by little, through the days, weeks, months and years, this child will have the kind of experiences that will produce the meanings that will make it possible for her eventually to understand the great words of our faith. The meanings that she will bring out of her experience will meet and be completed by the meanings that came out of the experience of men living under God; and the verbal and liturgical symbols, the words of our faith, will, indeed, be for her the words of life.

In baptism we promise to teach the child the Ten Commandments. And we pray in a closing prayer that this child, "being buried with Christ in his death, may also be partaker of his resurrection." What does this mean?

First, there is our responsibility to teach him the Ten

Commandments. The child needs the protection, guidance, and permissiveness of a disciplined relationship. He needs to obey as long as obedience is not required for obedience's sake alone. Without an ordered and disciplined framework, he becomes insecure and anxious. It is also true, though, that too much authority and too much required obedience will cause him to rebel with a hostility that will be like a poison in him. We will want to administer the law that is necesary to him in such a way that he will have its protection but at the same time leave him free to challenge its authority. Out of the inevitable struggle and resistance on the part of both himself and his parents, teachers, and others, he will discover himself in relation to law and begin to achieve some personal authority in relation to the authority of others.

In the process, however, he will discover that behind the rule (the law) stands a person (his parent) and that rebellion against the law is rebellion against the parent. Gradually, he will come to the insight that, inherent in every relationship, whether with man or God, is a law. And because he will resent the restraint of the law as seen in the demands of the person on him, he will resent the person; and when he acts against the restraint of the law and the demands of the person, he will become alienated from the person. So, we come to see that the law is necessary but that there is a terrible demand

and judgment implicit in it. The law destroys, and the only "adjustment" to authority is that which is effected and given to us by Christ who met with perfect obedience the full demand of the holiness of God.

These experiences will have to happen to him thousands and thousands of times as the child grows up and learns to live in relation to God and man. For both the child and the parent, some of the experiences are pretty grim. The conflict is real, the hostility is real, the alienation is real. But this is an inevitable experience for the parent who understands that through him and his relationship to his child, God seeks to confront the child with His truth; that the commandments of God have to be taught first through the language of relationship before the meaning of the words can be available to us.

When we undertake to teach in this way, we soon learn that we are involved in a good deal more than verbal activity. For instance, the mother in our story did not do something easy when she put her arm around her daughter and thus restored her to relationship. To do this, the mother had to die to her joy in a new dress, to her hurt and disappointment, to her desire to get even, to her illusions about herself, her daughter and their relationship to each other. In short, she had to bear the whole burden of the incident; but being buried with Christ in His death, she is able to restore the relationship because of His resurrected power working through her. And having lost her life, she finds it, because now she is available to her daughter as she never had been before. She has been raised up out of the loneliness and death of her relationship with her daughter. And so the truth of the prayer with which the service of baptism ends, that this child, "being buried with Christ in his death, may also be partaker of his resurrection" is being demonstrated by the faith-response of the mother to what God is trying to do through her. And the child out of this experience begins to learn what it means to die and be raised up and become in her turn an instrument of the saving work of God.

This is our faith, a faith not in myself and what I can do, nor in you and what you can do, nor in human institutions and what they can do, but in God and what He has done and is doing through the means He chooses. "I have been crucified with Christ; it is no longer I who live, but Christ who lives in me; and the life I now live in the flesh I live by faith in the Son of God, who loved me and gave himself for me." [2] What a wonderful privilege to be chosen as instruments of His redemption! But the great temptation is to believe that because we are an instrument of His redemption we are no longer in need of that same redemption.

[2] Gal. 2:20. From the Revised Standard Version of the Bible. Copyrighted 1946 and 1952.

When we forget our own need of redemption, we are in danger of holding a self-righteous, better-than-thou attitude which is a contradiction of the mind of Christ. The moment we lose our sense of need of redemption, in that moment and thereafter we cease to be instruments of redemption. When people say to us, "Why should I join the Church? Look at all the miserable sinners in it," we should respond, "Why, of course, Christ died for us, the Church is created for us and for you. Come on in!"

Our faith is an affirmation of our belief in God the Holy Spirit who brings into being this fellowship, this family, this people of God that has been given the task of bringing to the needs of men the reconciliation of God's love. Each relationship trembles with the promise of the realization of the presence and power of God. If we are open and responsive to Him, He speaks and acts through us, and we become the fellowship of the redeemed and the redeeming, the fellowship of the reconciled and the reconciling.

CHAPTER NINE

THE COMMUNION OF
THE HOLY COMMUNITY

WE ARE now ready to draw some conclusions from our study and to see some of its implications.

God is love. He created us in His own image to be persons living in personal relationship with Him, and in Him with one another. Our finiteness means, however, that to some degree we are and remain strangers to each other, separated and alone. In addition to all this, we use our freedom to say "no" to God, who is love and in whose image we were made. Our "no" puts us out of relationship with Him and each other so that our separation is made more desperate by our alienating way of living. And yet we were made for Him, for each other, for love. All men, therefore, are looking, whether they know it or not, for one who can reunite them with life, with Him in whom "we live and move and have our being." [1] Men have sought through the ages to bridge the separation, and to achieve reunion, but have succeeded only in showing the sincerity of their longing for reconciliation by the quality of their repentance.

[1] Acts 17:28.

But God being love did what only divine love could do. With the perfect grace of perfect love, He came to those whom He sought in the form in which they could receive Him. He came as a Person in historic encounter. We know Him as "Christ Jesus, who, though he was in the form of God, did not count equality with God a thing to be grasped, but emptied himself, taking the form of a servant, being born in the likeness of men. And being found in human form he humbled himself and became obedient unto death, even death on a cross. Therefore God has highly exalted him and bestowed on him the name which is above every other name, that at the name of Jesus every knee should bow, in heaven and on earth and under the earth, and every tongue confess that Jesus Christ is Lord, to the glory of God the Father." [2] And through Him God reconciled the world unto Himself.

And from the Father and the Son came the Spirit who makes us both new beings in His new creation and instruments for the completing of His work.

The Church is mankind redeemed in Christ. Not in the sense that we are without sin, but in the sense that we are His and our fellowship is with Him, and we depend upon Him to do for us what we cannot do for ourselves. His Spirit dwells among us, between man

[2] 1 Philippians 2:6-11. From the Revised Standard Version of the Bible. Copyrighted 1946 and 1952.

and man, you and me, and "the help that He gives is only available at the level of the fullest possible personal relationship and reciprocal communion." [3] We exist not only to enjoy His gifts but to take them to others in the same person-to-person encounter. The gift is a *new* relationship, the relationship of reconciliation that we have with one another and God in Christ. The Church, therefore, is the whole company of those who share in His reconciliation.

The sacrament of Holy Baptism is both the instrument of the Church's being and the door through which we individually enter into that fellowship of reconciled and reconciling men. When we look at life in the Church, we have to make two comments. First, because of our new relationship with God in Christ through our baptism, we are cleansed from sin and saved from death. Second, we must "walk worthily" of this calling into a new relationship, recognizing within us and the world that which drives us to break and destroy the fellowship. While there is conflict within each of us between what we are in Christ (at one with God and man) and what we do of ourselves (words and acts of alienation), the conflict does not make us anxious and guilty in ways that will destroy us. Many people regard this conflict as an unendurable contradiction and will

[3] J. E. Fison, *The Blessings of the Holy Spirit.* (New York, Longmans, Green, 1950), p. 146. Used by permission of the publisher.

have nothing to do with the Church or its people because of it. Their difficulty is that they can accept neither God *nor* man; it is a part of the human need to see everything as either black or white. Instead, man is both saint and sinner. He can say "yes" and "no," and love and hate at the same time. Therefore, a Christian is one who can both praise God for salvation and confess that he is a sinner without being surprised or dismayed. We can accept ourselves because God accepts us and loves us, and we can accept and love one another, too. There is nothing heroic about this. Instead there is only a quiet acceptance of a trusting way of living together in spite of every contrary and destructive force.

Some years ago six men waited with quiet matter-of-factness in a penitentiary warden's office for their friend who, after a year's imprisonment, was to be released. He had been a trusted member of the governing body of his church when he was tried, convicted, and sentenced. Although it had not been easy to accept him and his guilt, these men, who had been his colleagues in the church, together with their minister had kept in touch with him. He had not known that they were going to be there to receive him, but they knew that he would need help. When he came out, they *were* there and *received* him with the reassurances of their love and confidence in him. With this strength he was able to begin to rebuild his life. His experiences during the next few years were often discouraging, but he was sustained by their faith in him and their acceptance of him. They witnessed to the love and acceptance of God and were instruments of them, too.

The Holy Spirit thus creates the community without which the new relationship can not endure. We call it a *holy* community because it is a fellowship of God and man, and the life we have from God is holy. Unfortunately, many of us think that the primary meaning of holy is moral perfection; but we are holy and our relationships are holy, not because of our moral perfection but because of our relation to the Holy God who cleanses, unites, completes, and fulfills all in Himself. We are never holy of ourselves, but we rejoice that the Spirit of the Holy One is working among us and others to make us and our relationship holy. The Christian ethic is never one of personal accomplishment, but is always personal response, the response of gratitude to the holy and loving God. Through Holy Baptism, therefore, we are born into a Holy Community because of our relation to our Holy God.

What is our relation to God? In view of all that we have learned thus far, we should conclude that our relation to God is one of gratitude for His acceptance and love, of praise and thanksgiving for restoration of relationship. For this reason the people of God assemble together to give corporate expression of their gratitude in worship. Christian people through the centuries have felt that their worship could most adequately be expressed through the Holy Communion or the Lord's Supper, in which we remember God's saving acts (chiefly our Saviour's death and resurrection) by which He meets our need. In response we offer His death and sacrifice for us and with it offer ourselves, our souls and bodies, and make our offering of praise and thanksgiving. The Holy Community, initiated by Holy Baptism, is thus renewed by Holy Communion. Holy Communion is also a relationship phrase: Communion means "union with." In Holy Communion we may participate in the reunion of the separated and the reconciliation of the alienated. We may experience a renewing of at-oneness that makes it possible for us to offer men a relationship of love and acceptance in which God's gift of reconciliation will be more readily recognized and received.

The direction of our Christian witness and service, therefore, should not be back to the Church from which it sprang, but from the Church to the community. The Church is not meant to be the object of salvation but an instrument of it. The test is not in what I do for my church but what I do as a member of the Church in the political, social, economic, educational, recreational life of the world. Unless the vitality born of the meeting between God and men in worship finds expression in the issues of living, then personal relations, individual or social, are doomed. And the Church (you and I, all of us) because of neurotic preoccupation with her own welfare will be responsible.

The reunion and renewal of the Holy Community concerns more than the human world. It speaks of reconciliation not only between men but between men and things, between nature and human nature. The elements of bread and wine (things) become the instruments of reunion so that men may participate again in the true relation of person to person and things to things; namely, to love persons and use things.

The relationship of worship, of which prayer is a part, is the renewing of relationship. Sacraments, as we have seen, are the means of God's action, but prayer is the means of our response. Many people today find prayer unreal and do not pray. There are many reasons for this that cannot be listed and discussed now, but chief among them is that we are apt to think of prayer as being a separate, specialized, verbalizing activity.

In contrast to this concept, prayer is meeting, and being in relation with God and, no less, man. We have already seen that all men want to be in relation as fully as possible, to have someone with whom they can be at one and who can be at one with them and through whom they can find at-oneness with all. If prayer is seeking to be in relation, then we all, in one way or another, to some degree or other, are praying and trying to pray.

The concept of prayer as the practice of relationship becomes clearer when we think of it in terms of the five kinds of prayer: adoration, confession, petition, intercession, and thanksgiving. When we stop to think about it, these words describe five kinds of relationships that are essential to any real personal meeting with God and, in Him, of man with man. Adoration is giving ourselves to another in love and honest admiration. Confession is the acceptance and acknowledgment of our words and acts of alienation. Petition is an acknowledgment of our dependence on one another. Intercession is the expression of our responsibility to live for and to help one another. And thanksgiving is the expression of our gratitude for fellowship and all other blessings.

Prayer, then, is choosing to respond to God's reconciling love for us. Prayer is an act of love; it is choosing to meet God and man and to live in mutual relation with them. Prayer is losing one's egocentric life and receiving it back cleansed and renewed and capable of enjoying the fellowship of God and man. And prayer is the practice of our new relationship for the sake of all men who are killing themselves and each other for want of Him who would receive them unto Himself.

Finally, the worship of the Holy Community in Holy Communion provides us with a foretaste of the consummation of God's saving work. In the last day, all who have responded to the gift of the new relationship in Christ will have that relationship fulfilled; then they will see, not dimly but face-to-face. Then the work of acceptance, love, and discipline will have been completed. Then the needs of men will be fully answered not by the action of God but by the meeting with God Himself.

Men fear death as they fear loneliness, meaninglessness, non-being. We seek reassurance for the unknown future; some evidence that our fears are groundless. We cannot offer blueprints and maps of a celestial and heavenly city; but God has given us Someone who will meet us there. We know Him. His name is Jesus. We call Him Christ our Lord. He gave us the new relationship with the promise that we could count on Him. "When I go and prepare a place for you, I will come again and will take you to myself, that where I am you may be also." [4]

In the assurance of the Saviour Himself we turn with new courage to the life we are living. We are a people sent to live in the present, to learn the lessons and to do the work of our day, witnessing to Him who gives it all its full meaning and the promise of its consummation. We are a people who live in hope. We rejoice

[4] John 14:3. From the Revised Standard Version of the Bible. Copyrighted 1946 and 1952.

in the good of the present but we have no illusions
about ourselves and our relations to one another; otherwise we would have no sense of our need of a saviour.
But the great and final meaning of our new relationship in Christ is that it is permanent. It is eternal, and
is not limited by time or space. The fellowship of the
new relationship holds communion that breaks down
the barriers of past, present, and future. When our life
is hid with Christ in God, we are in communion and,
therefore, in relationship with all men of all time and
beyond time—with all creation. Therefore:

I consider that the sufferings of this present time are not
worth comparing with the glory that is to be revealed to us.
For the creation waits with eager longing for the revealing
of the sons of God; for the creation was subjected to futility,
not of its own will but by the will of him who subjected it
in hope; because the creation itself will be set free from its
bondage to decay and obtain the glorious liberty of the children of God.[5]

[5] Rom. 8:18-21. From the Revised Standard Version of the Bible.
Copyrighted 1946 and 1952.

INDEX